# WHY
# FASHION
# MATTERS

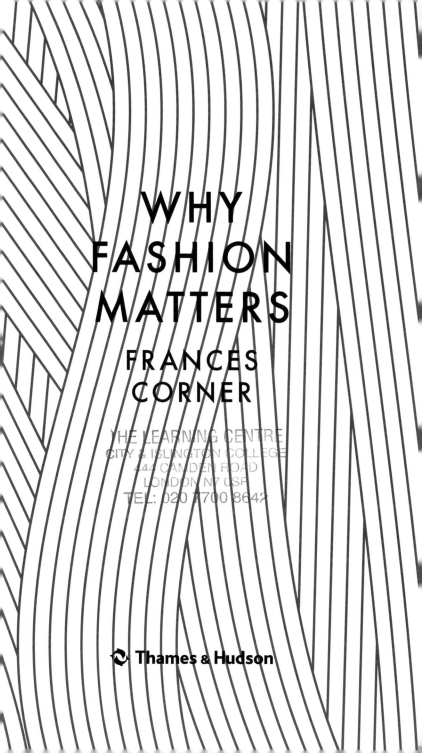

# WHY FASHION MATTERS

## FRANCES CORNER

Thames & Hudson

# INTRODUCTION

Fashion matters.
To the economy, to
society and to each of
us personally. Faster
than anything else,
what we wear tells
the story of who we
are – or who we want
to be. Fashion is the
most immediate and
intimate form of
self-expression.

Yet even as fashion touches the lives of each and every one of us, its influence and the vast creative industry that it supports can seem mysterious. With this book of 101 bite-sized reflections, I have set out to explain why fashion matters and to sketch out its increasing influence on lives and industries around the globe.

Fashion is a multi-billion dollar industry that employs a whole host of professionals, including designers, manufacturers, garment workers, retailers, hair stylists, make-up artists, merchandisers, journalists, photographers and models. Fashion provides millions of people worldwide with their livelihoods and builds commercial ties between nations. Goods designed in one country are often manufactured in another, before being shipped and sold in many more countries around the world.

Like most other global industries, fashion has its dark side. Eating disorders, a lack of ethnic representation, water and resource depletion and the exploitation of vulnerable garment workers are only a few of the issues that the industry must do more to address and resolve. Consumers too must do more.

Fashion deserves to be taken seriously, warts and all, and celebrated for its beauty, creativity and entrepreneurial spirit. The fashion industry is among the most aspirational, industrious and dynamic of all industries. Its best designers, as with all great artists, imagine, initiate and move culture on. The cut or pattern that first appeared on the catwalk soon finds its way onto store shelves and into our wardrobes. Whether or not we like to admit it, what we wear and how we wear it is inevitably influenced by designers' ideas and creative decisions.

At heart, fashion is all about the art of self-adornment: the visual presentation of ourselves to the external world. What we choose to wear reflects how we view the world and how we want the world to view us. The prehistoric caveman with the latest beads, the post-war woman in Dior's New Look, the latest fashion blog recording street style as it happens – they are all tied to our very human need to express individuality.

Fashion has been and always will be a constant part of our existence. Why?

Because fashion really does matter.

101
THOUGHTS
ON

# WHY
# FASHION
# MATTERS

# THE COUTURE LABORATORY

**1** I attended my first haute couture show soon after starting as Head of London College of Fashion. I was determined to gain an understanding of these special collections and the incomparable skills of the ateliers that craft them entirely by hand. I was not disappointed; they are extraordinary.

Haute couture was developed in France to protect Paris's status as the world's fashion capital. Even today, what does and does not qualify as couture is strictly governed by the Chambre Syndicale de la Haute Couture, a trade organization with roots in the nineteenth century. Many people confuse haute couture with the ready-to-wear collections covered extensively in the media but couture is quite distinct. For a fashion house to qualify as a maker of couture it must follow strict rules: it must design made-to-order garments for private clients, with one or more fittings necessary, maintain a workshop in Paris that employs at least fifteen people full-time, and show two collections each year in Paris in January and July, with each one comprised of at least thirty-five outfits for both day- and eveningwear.

To some, couture is an anachronism, elitist and irrelevant. But I admire it as a system that has preserved and protected a vast range of skills and crafts, such as fine embroidery, beadwork and the decorative use of feathers or precious stones. Many of these skills are no longer practised anywhere else in the world, making Paris the global centre for the creation of these exquisite, handmade, one-off fashions.

In the 1990s, it seemed as if couture might be dying because not enough clients were regularly buying sufficient quantities to keep the ateliers alive. Now, with the growth of wealth in Russia, Asia and the Middle East, couture is once again flourishing, so much so that Giorgio Armani and Dolce & Gabbana have added it to their repertoire in recent years. The Chambre Syndicale has also embraced new foreign-born couturiers, including Livia Stoianova and Yassen Samoilov of On Aura Tout Vu, Rad Hourani, Laurence Xu and Didit Hediprasetyo, all of whom have brought new vitality to this traditional French industry.

In the end, couture is all about the beauty of the clothes. As my colleague Tony Glenville, who introduced me to all things couture, has said: 'In spite of rumours of the demise of couture, the snide comments from people who say it is PR only to sell fragrance and those who see no modern validity in it, it survives. It is where art and fashion meet if only briefly. . . . It is still a laboratory for design and things are possible in couture which are impossible anywhere else.'

# CLOSING THE (PLASTIC BOTTLE) LOOP

**2** The idea that plastic bottles can be recycled into other objects, saving them from the landfill, has captured the imaginations of many. Making new clothes from old bottles is thought to consume less energy than standard polyester production and a number of major retailers are turning to recycled textiles to 'green' their supply chain. As with all environmental issues, the reality is more complicated. Manufacturing polyester from recycled bottles may consume less energy than manufacturing new polyester from fossil fuels but it consumes more energy than is necessary to produce organic natural fibres. Melting and re-extruding the plastic to make new yarns also degrades it so that eventually it can no longer be recycled. As the base colours of the recycled plastic vary in consistency, more chemical dye is necessary to achieve a uniform colour. Fabrics made from synthetic and organic blends cannot be recycled at all.

Achieving a closed loop of production in which yarns can be recycled indefinitely seems a long way off but there has been progress. Some companies are designing products that do not feature backings or use textile blends. Textile manufacturers are beginning to create more fabrics without the carcinogenic chemical antimony, which can be released into the environment through wastewater. Significant research is going into the fabrication of bio-based polymers that will be recyclable, biodegradable and made from sustainable sources. Such fabrics would have the positive properties of any conventional synthetic material, including its low cost of manufacture, but none of the negative side effects.

# THE 'CLOTHES THAT WEAR US'

**3** One of my favourite fashion books is Colin McDowell's *Literary Companion to Fashion*. Covering over four hundred years of literature from Britain, Ireland, Europe and America, it explores the rituals and meanings of dress, as well as the intrinsic role that clothes play in the creation of character and the telling of a story that is both believable and meaningful.

Whenever I revisit this book, I find myself reflecting on stories, novels and plays that I have personally read or seen performed. From fairy tales such as Little Red Riding Hood, Cinderella, The Emperor's New Clothes and The Elves and the Shoemaker to the novels of Marcel Proust, Doris Lessing and Jean Rhys, the importance placed upon clothes and accessories in these texts is remarkable and moving.

For me, it is a passage from Virginia Woolf's novel *Orlando*, in which the central protagonist shifts gender halfway through, that most brilliantly articulates the significance of clothes in both our lives and those of characters:

'THERE IS MUCH TO SUPPORT THE VIEW THAT IT IS CLOTHES THAT WEAR US, AND NOT WE, THEM; WE MAY MAKE THEM TAKE THE MOULD OF ARM OR BREAST, BUT THEY MOULD OUR HEARTS, OUR BRAINS, OUR TONGUES TO THEIR LIKING.'

# PRADA, ZARA AND THE GREAT MARK-UP MYSTERY

**4** Did you know that of any industry fashion has the greatest range of stages involved in the making of its products? Its supply chain is long and convoluted, often involving travel between factories and countries, contractors and subcontractors. Partly because of this complexity, fashion has a greater range of mark-ups than any other industry.

Now that we're all happy to mix our Prada with our Zara, we tend to have little to no understanding of the true value of each garment or accessory in our wardrobes. Designer labels and high-street retailers often use the same factories and labourers, yet they attach wildly different price tags to their goods. Counterfeiting and cheap copies take shoppers further and further away from the reality of production costs. You would hope that a higher price tag guaranteed that the garment worker who made it received a living wage, but too often it doesn't. How can value and price begin to reflect one another once again?

# THE AFRICAN
# LUXURY MARKET

**5** Africa is being touted as the next Asia with regards to retail and a growing consumer appetite for luxury goods. *The International Herald Tribune*'s 2012 Luxury Conference was dedicated to discussing the potential for Africa to be both a 'producer and ultimately consumer of luxury goods'.

Seven of the world's ten fastest growing economies are in Africa and seventy per cent of the continent's population live in countries that have enjoyed annual economic growth of over four per cent in the past decade. Approximately 310 million Africans are now middle-class and eager to buy local fashions that epitomize excellence. While for the majority of the continent's people, poverty remains a cruel reality, according to a report from *The Economist*'s Intelligence Unit, Africa's eighteen leading national economies will have a combined spending power of $1.3 trillion by 2030.

Across Africa there is a real hunger for and interest in fashion and the creative industries. With the numbers of fifteen to twenty-five year olds increasing significantly, the desire for Western fashion is growing at an exponential rate and brand awareness is becoming very sophisticated. Zara, Nike, Levi's and Gap have all recently opened stores in either South Africa, Kenya, Ghana or Nigeria. Luxury brand Ermenegildo Zegna has pioneered the opening of a number of high-end stores across the continent.

Fashion weeks in Lagos, Nigeria, and Accra, Ghana, are working to raise the profile of African fashion across the continent, while designers are pioneering their own contributions to the burgeoning fashion industry, often absorbing Western cultural references before twisting and changing them to suit local styles. Traditional artisanal skills and craftsmanship are often key to the production of these new designs, resulting in garments that are highly desirable to African consumers as well as a global audience looking for something fresh and authentic. How African fashion and traditional dress may fuse and intertwine over the coming years seems likely to lead to all sorts of creative possibilities and tensions. Watch this space.

# EDUCATION, EXPERIMENTATION AND ATTITUDE

**6** Since 2005 I have enjoyed the privilege of being Head of the London College of Fashion, one of the world's leading fashion education institutions since its founding in 1906. Perhaps unsurprisingly, the importance and value of education is something to which I have devoted quite a lot of thought.

Education should give students the opportunity to test, experiment, investigate and undergo a series of experiences that ultimately transform their thinking, like some form of alchemy, about the world around them. Education should equip them with the confidence and abilities to shape their own lives, to plan and to respond to challenges in ways that were previously inconceivable to them.

Hope combined with the belief that there is a way through every problem is at the heart of the creative process. Over the years, I have tried to build this attitude and approach into the courses of every educational institution at which I have worked. At the heart of this philosophy is the journey, both physical and intellectual. This journey cannot be precisely planned because, while you might know your destination, both anticipated and unanticipated obstacles are bound to arise.

There are countless ways to achieve your goal, whatever that may be. A flexibility in thought will give you the courage to seize whatever opportunities come your way without losing sight of your true aim. This flexibility should extend to what the end result may be, not as an excuse for under achievement but in recognition that as we grow and change, so too will what we want out of life.

Openness, flexibility, curiosity and the conviction that for every decision made an equally interesting, difficult or adventurous option could have been taken, these are the qualities that should motivate every creative graduate. John Cage greatly influenced my thoughts on education. He worked as an artist, composer, chess player and mushroom expert – whatever seemed right at any given moment in his thinking and creativity.

That hunger for experimentation and knowledge is critical to achieving great things in every area of the arts and education. Many of my female influences have taken similar approaches. Simone de Beauvoir, Frida Kahlo and Julia Kristeva all pushed or push the boundaries of their disciplines, challenging existing knowledge and conventions, and inspiring us all to achieve great things whatever the difficulties.

# QUESTION

If all art was once contemporary, were all clothes once fashionable?

# CORSETS TO CRINOLINES, BOTOX TO DIETING

**8** Throughout history, across cultures and trends, constraint and constriction have been constant features of women's dress. The higher the status of the woman – or more to the point, the status of her husband or family – the more physically restrictive her clothing. The tightly laced corsets of eighteenth- and nineteenth-century Europe slimmed waists down to tiny proportions – often at the expense of a woman's ability to breathe. In China, until the early twentieth century, many young girls had their toes broken and each foot bound tightly so that their feet would stay forever stunted. Their tiny, deformed feet were considered symbolic of their families' wealth since these women would never be able to work and had to employ servants to undertake all manual tasks.

It may seem that the twenty-first-century emphasis on freedom and individuality has brought about more sensible and empowering dress, such as sportswear, Lycra, trainers, leggings and sweatshirts, and that we are less constrained by fashion than ever before. But the opposite is true too. Stiletto heels and oversized platforms are obvious examples. I also think that extreme dieting and exercise have taken over as the latest means to constrict us into fashion. From corsets, foot binding, crinolines and farthingales to skinny jeans, waxing, facelifts and Botox, the effort, time and money needed to achieve the perfect look remains as restrictive as ever.

# THE REAL
# FASHION VICTIMS

**9** The majority of new clothes, whether luxury or mass-market, are manufactured in Asian factories. Doing so keeps costs low and margins high. Bangladesh has a minimum wage of $38 a month making it particularly attractive to many retailers and brands. It also has appallingly lax health and safety laws. Vulnerable garment workers – eighty per cent of whom are women – work long hours in substandard facilities, without benefits and for little compensation. According to a 2012 report from the International Labor Rights Forum, over one thousand garment workers have been killed since 1990 in preventable factory fires. Corruption is rife and since factory owners make up some ten per cent of the Bangladeshi parliament the consequences for criminal negligence are few.

On 24 April 2013, just outside Dhaka, Bangladesh's capital city, the eight-storey Rana Plaza factory collapsed, killing over 1,100 garment workers and injuring over 2,500 more. Extensive media coverage and outrage around the world helped the Clean Clothes Campaign and global union Industriall convince many Western brands and retailers to sign the enforceable Accord on Fire and Building Safety, which should improve the working conditions in all Bangladeshi factories. More than seventy foreign companies, from Primark to Abercrombie & Fitch, signed the accord in the three months following the accident, a huge step forward in creating better working conditions for Bangladeshi garment workers. But other companies refused.

How many avoidable tragedies will it take before all retailers demand the fair and safe treatment of these workers? Again and again, the fashion and garment industries fail to take responsibility for these very real fashion victims. So too, we as consumers must hold ourselves accountable for our purchases. For many garment workers, a living wage is only a few pennies away; pennies that for us are just spare change.

# PARIS CHIC, LONDON COOL, SHANGHAI STYLE

**10** Firmly established as a major manufacturing centre for the fashion industry, China is also a nation of avid fashion consumers. In 2012, China bypassed the United States to become the largest national market for luxury goods in the world. Its growing middle class and increased exposure to the West through global tourism have contributed to this incredible expansion. In the past few years, the 'logo-mania' of the 2000s has ceded territory to more understated but no less luxurious product as Chinese consumers have become more sophisticated in their tastes. The emphasis has shifted from prominent brand names to more discreet luxury labels that are still recognizable to those 'in the know'.

WESTERN FASHION BRANDS HAVE BEEN QUICK TO ADJUST THEIR MARKETING AND PRODUCTS TO CHANGES IN TASTE, BUT SO TOO HAVE CHINESE FASHION BRANDS AND LABELS.

China is no longer interested in just manufacturing and consuming fashion; it wants to be a force for designing original fashion too.

I heard the Chinese economist Li Wuwei, author of *How Creativity is Changing China*, speak about how the economic transformation of China into a creative, design-led economy may come about. An adviser to the Chinese government, he touched on a number of Chinese heritage brands, including a 1930s cosmetic company and a Shanghai vinegar company, as examples of high-end businesses that have effectively repositioned themselves as part of the luxury sector through new ideas, products, design and packaging. By maximizing their value chains through vertical integration, extending the brand to new products and combining product development with the cultural desires of the consumer, Li argued that other Chinese businesses could be similarly successful.

Neither a Chinese fashion house nor a Chinese retailer has yet achieved substantial international recognition or sales. But never say never. Menswear label Bosideng opened its first Western flagship on London's Bond Street in 2013 and had plans to open soon after on New York's Fifth Avenue. It may be the first of many, many more.

# THE TORTOISE AND THE HARE

**11** Slow or fast? Tortoise or hare? A split seems to be developing in the fashion industry. First up, dashing ahead to take the lead, fast fashion: the straight-to-market, trend-led product created for mass consumption at the lowest possible price and meant to be worn for no more than a season. In last place, bringing up the rear, slow fashion: the luxury, bespoke and high-end approach that puts an emphasis on quality not quantity, timelessness not trends. In the middle, a beleaguered business model lingers. Unable to achieve the rapidity of fast fashion or the endurance and fine craftsmanship of slow luxury, it is being squeezed out of the race altogether. I'm not sure what animal that might be. The dodo?

# THE DEMISE OF THE FASHION DICTATOR

**12** Throughout the twentieth century, the structure of the fashion industry, the media and society as a whole made it possible for a single designer to dictate what was and was not fashionable. Coco Chanel, Christian Dior, Mary Quant and Yves Saint Laurent are just a few of the designers who exerted this influence at some point in their careers and designed clothes that fundamentally changed the way that women dressed. Even in the last two decades of the twentieth century, designers with a singular vision could have a major impact: Issey Miyake's experimentation with fabrics had a knock-on effect on all fashion textiles; Thierry Mugler's lavishly staged fashion shows made the intermingling of fashion and performance a given.

Times have changed. In our now interdependent world, no one individual – and no one fashion capital – has the clout to change the way a whole subsection of society dresses. Hemlines no longer drop or rise because one designer says they should. New York, London, Dubai and Tokyo now vie with Paris as influential fashion cities. Fashion bibles *Vogue* and *Harper's Bazaar* now share readers with *AnOther Magazine* and *Love*, not to mention any number of blogs. Street style influences couture even as couture influences street style.

Simply put, there is no longer one look or way to be fashionable. Around the world, fashion-conscious men and women now have easy, near-instant access to a myriad of styles at a variety of price bands. Even more to the point, with the quick upload of their latest looks these same men and women can now dictate to the dictators just what is and isn't fashionable. The democratization of fashion is well underway. Long may it reign.

# SINGING THE DENIM BLUES

**13** Jeans began life as a utility garment because of the hardwearing nature of the fabric, yet from their origins as the informal uniform of America's Gold Rush and timber industry, they have evolved into a stylish staple that features on catwalks and in high-end fashion magazines. A good pair of jeans can last a lifetime, their durability matched by a flexibility that means they quickly mould to fit one's shape. Many of us regard our favourite pair of jeans as a familiar friend associated with key moments in our lives.

Many of us also have multiple pairs of jeans. According to a Cotton Inc. survey, the average American woman owns 8.3 pairs. In 2007, research anticipated that the British were set to spend some £1.51 billion on eighty-six million pairs of jeans. Jeans can now be bought at every price point, in every colour and in innumerable styles. They have come a long way from their origins as the working man's uniform.

> While jeans could appear to be an ideal example of sustainable fashion, they actually exemplify the darker side of clothing production. Jeans are made from cotton, which needs large amounts of land and even larger amounts of pesticides to grow. Achieving that blue-denim rinse requires numerous dyeing processes that consume huge amounts of water. According to Levi's, over three thousand litres of water will be used during the full product lifecycle of a single pair of 501 jeans, from the cotton production and manufacturing processes to their regular washing at home.

Since the 1980s, jeans have often been designed to appear pre-worn, a look achieved by sandblasting, which has led to many garment workers contracting the incurable lung disease silicosis. In Turkey, where the backlash against sandblasting first began, there have been 1,200 registered cases of silicosis, though many doctors believe the number to be much higher. In Bangladesh, where there are some four thousand garment-making factories, jeans production employs thousands. Employees often work eleven hours a day for as little as $38 a month – the living wage in Bangladesh is $100 a month – in conditions where the air is filled with tiny particles of silica. A number of companies have moved to ban sandblasting, including Levi's, H&M and C&A. Versace and Gucci have also made a commitment to stop using the process in the manufacturing of jeans. The clothing industry's reliance on subcontractors, however, makes it difficult to enforce such bans. One way to end the practice of sandblasting jeans would be to create our own wear and tear. Who else remembers using a pumice stone to soften up a new pair of jeans and make them look worn-in?

# THE ADVANTAGE OF VINTAGE

**14** At what point in the history of an item of clothing does pre-worn become second-hand, become retro, become vintage? Recycling clothes and buying clothes that have had at least one previous owner is vital for an environmentally sustainable future. Luckily, the preference for vintage has caught on and vintage clothes are now a key part of every fashionable person's wardrobe. Vintage has become such big business that in the United States thirty-five tonnes of second-hand printed T-shirts are sorted everyday and eight million kilos of second-hand clothes are sold for export every year.

THE ORGANIC RE-BRANDING OF SECOND-HAND CLOTHES AS VINTAGE FASHION IS NO BAD THING FOR THE ENVIRONMENT AND I HOPE THAT THE TREND WILL LAST.

Let's be on guard for cynical marketing ploys that try to undermine or debase the vintage label. Whatever name it goes by, the passing on and reusing of clothes reduces our consumption of newly manufactured goods. After all, one man's rags are another man's riches.

# 15

# QUESTION: PIPE DREAMS

If fashion is selling us a dream, why does it make us feel so inadequate? Is the fashion industry preying on our insecurities under the guise of trying to make us fashionable?

# CARMEN DELL'OREFICE: A MODEL EXAMPLE

**16** In an industry obsessed with youth and change, most models rarely last more than a few seasons. Carmen Dell'Orefice is the exception. At over eighty years old, she is far more than just a face; she understands that in this forever shifting industry it is critical to know who you are. 'Fashion is part of communication. It's the beginning. We describe part of ourselves by how we look, but you can't tell a book by its cover. There's an appropriateness. I think it's funny when decades and things are just the current thing. . . . Everybody wants to be somebody else, rather than using those images as a stimulation to look at themselves and redefine and redesign themselves and see who they are.'

For many, Carmen is an inspiration who has challenged assumptions and boundaries at every stage of her life and career. She understood early that her looks could transform a bleak and impoverished childhood during which her single mother had to put her in foster care while raising enough rent to house the two of them. At thirteen, Carmen posed topless for Salvador Dalí for $12 an hour. Two years later, in 1947, she appeared on the cover of *Vogue*. She went on to grace the cover of *Vogue* five times, to pose for Irving Penn, Cecil Beaton, Richard Avedon, Horst P. Horst and John Rawlings, and to front fourteen cosmetics campaigns.

Carmen retired briefly in 1966 at the age of thirty-five but soon returned for her 'second phase'. While continuing to work with established photographers, this time she was also fêted by a new generation that included Nick Knight and Helmut Newton. The industry had changed and models were no longer 'coat-hangers' but professionals in their own right who photographers collaborated with and looked to for inspiration. This is the point in Carmen's career when her contribution to the industry becomes so clear. In each photograph, she translates and transforms both the clothes and the vision of the photographer into a reality that is more than just a fashion shoot.

Carmen understands the shapes, structure, setting and lighting, and how hair, make-up and clothes all combine with her face to create the perfect image. Of her own thought processes during a shoot, she has said: 'I've always appreciated what [the photographer's] job is, what they're trying to do. I'm just part of the picture. I'm not the picture. There's so much that goes into it, you know? It's got to be a team effort. Think about family. Think about living. My goal in life is to do better than "Do no harm." How do you do some good that really hits the mark? Well, you start one smile at a time, one overt little thing to make another human being know that you notice them, that you feel for them, that you're happy when they're happy.'

# VIVA ITALIA

**17** According to an Elliott Morss report on data published in 2008, developed nations spend about four per cent of their consumption expenditure on clothing, except for Italy, which spends double that at eight per cent. In comparison, developed nations spend ten per cent on recreation and culture, and eight per cent on restaurants and hotels. The United States imports twenty-two per cent of its clothing and this amount is likely to increase by up to ten per cent following the removal of the Chinese clothing and textile import quota. In contrast, Italy imports only five per cent of its clothes. In spending more but importing less, Italians support their domestic economy by wearing, as well as making, Italian fashion.

# ARTICULATE BY DESIGN

**18** Just as the clothes we wear are visual manifestations of our inner selves, so too the words and phrases that we use are verbal embodiments of fashion's far-reaching influence. Language first used only in the context of dressing and undressing, or the making and marketing of clothes, has over time found its way into everyday speech. Uniform, tailored, armour, crease, fold, seamless, baggy, loose, ill-fitting, stitched-up, overdressed – these are just some of the words through which the language of fashion articulates so many other aspects of the world and our lives.

# 19

FACT:
A LONGER
LIFE

If we all extended the use of a garment by nine months – which according to studies would mean making it last three years – we could save $8 billion a year on the cost of resources used to manufacture, launder and dispose of clothing. The carbon, water and waste footprints of our clothes would be reduced by twenty to thirty per cent. Surely nine months isn't too much to ask?

# ARE MEN THE
# NEW WOMEN?

**20** Over the course of the eighteenth century, a seismic shift occurred in how European men dressed. Then as now, dress communicated status and was a means to display your position in society. *What* men wore, however, was until this point markedly different from present-day menswear. For centuries, men's dress had been as elaborate, expensive, embellished and rich in texture as any women's garment, sometimes even more so.

But a countermovement against ostentatious dress was underway. The influence of Enlightenment thought, with its interest and commitment to science, rational thinking and education rather than social status, was spreading. Colourful fabrics and heavy jewelry were on their way out, replaced by more practical, sober suits and a strict dress code for every occasion. The Great Male Renunciation had begun to gain ground.

Of course, many men still cared just as much about fashion as women, so even as these individuals conformed to the new masculine uniform, they continued to find ways to indicate their fashion-forwardness. Beau Brummell, friend to the Prince Regent in the 1790s and early 1800s, became the standard for elegance and refinement in dress. He put the emphasis on cut and detail so that the tie of one's cravat could indicate your status, much the same as the most luxurious, embroidered silk cloak had centuries before. Brummell is often dubbed the first dandy, but being a dandy was always about more than clothes. As Baudelaire wrote: 'Contrary to what many thoughtless people seem to believe, dandyism is not even an excessive delight in clothes and material elegance. For the perfect dandy, these things are no more than the symbol of the aristocratic superiority of his mind.' The dandy's minimal but perfectionist approach to fashion touched all other aspects of his life, including elegance in manners, discourse and grooming.

The dandy of the nineteenth and first half of the twentieth century essentially kept to the male uniform of trousers, shirt and jacket. Sartorial experimentation rarely extended beyond accessories or detailing. Then came the Peacocks of the 1960s in their brightly coloured bellbottomed suits and patterned shirts and you could be forgiven for thinking that permanent change in menswear was at hand. Yet that look turned out to be a trend that soon fizzled out.

At the moment, there is a real sense of experimentation in menswear. Young designers are embracing flamboyant colours, textures and digital prints – and crucially, you can actually spot men wearing these creations. A recent report from the consultancy Bain & Company quantified my hunch when it identified the growth of menswear at fourteen per cent – almost double that of womenswear.

MAYBE WE ARE BEGINNING TO SEE A RESURGENCE OF FAR GREATER INDIVIDUALITY IN MENSWEAR. COULD THE GREAT MALE RENAISSANCE BE UPON US?

In previous generations, being a dandy was primarily about expressing a certain philosophy, whereas today I would argue that there are broader social, economic and cultural forces at play, including a more open society that supports greater freedom of expression for men, the power of the 'pink dollar', the move away from conventional office wear and work places, and the growth in blogs, magazines, fashion collections and fashion weeks that are dedicated to all things male.

# SPACE AGE STYLE

**21** In thinking about ideas or innovations that were ahead of their time, it is tempting to focus on those that had a momentous impact on our day-to-day living. The wheel, the printing press, the Internet and even the smart phone all altered our lives radically in ways that can never be reversed. Sometimes these inventions were instantaneous in their adoption; others took more time for people to see their true value.

How does this relate to clothing and the ordinary garments that we wear everyday? Fashion promotes itself as ever evolving and adapting, but in reality most items of clothing have changed little over the years. Radical new developments in the last fifty years have changed some of the fabrics we wear but the futuristic fashions of the 1960s, as dreamt up by Pierre Cardin, André Courrèges and Paco Rabanne, still seem a long way off. Where are the inventions and radical ideas in fashion? Maybe the future challenge for the fashion industry will be how to integrate the technologies that have become so much a part of our lives with what we wear.

# FASHION AS ECOSYSTEM

**22** I am often asked for advice by visitors from overseas on how best they can develop their own fashion industries and educational institutions. What are the main building blocks? To them, and now to you, I always say: fashion needs an ecosystem.

AT THE HEART OF EVERY SUCCESSFUL FASHION ECONOMY LIES A CONCENTRATED GROUP OF ENTHUSIASTS WHO ARE BOTH PERFORMERS AND AUDIENCE TO ONE ANOTHER.

If fashion needs an ecosystem, that ecosystem requires a city in order to thrive. Only there will fashion find its audience and the resources to sustain it, not least the creativity and ambition of the individuals drawn into this urban orbit. A fashion ecosystem needs a range of retailers, a strong youth culture, museums, galleries and other cultural institutions. It needs street style and professional stylists, the fashion media and all the editors, journalists, bloggers, photographers and illustrators that go with it. It also needs skilled design talent, merchandisers, machinists and manufacturers small and large, producing diverse and innovative materials and fabrics. It needs popular culture and the expressive individualism that thrives in crowded streets, bars and restaurants. It needs consumers who want to be part of the fashion pack as well as in the fashion vanguard. Creating a fashion ecosystem takes time, energy and human desire but it can be done.

# 23

# QUESTION

If fashion is ephemeral and superficial, what does that say about us? Like clothes, we fade and decay. Are we too just another type of ephemera or are we more than that?

# THE RIGHT
# TO BUY

**24** Stop buying, we are told. Stop purchasing so many cheap clothes only to throw them away months later.

The assumption behind these commands seems to be that if only we could show a bit more self-control and deny ourselves the pleasure of the new, we would soon reduce the problem of over-consumption – or, at the very least, salve our guilty consciences. But it is unrealistic to think we can turn back the clock to a time when shopping was not a central part of our day-to-day existence. Simply put, we love to shop and we love to buy, so much so that new clothes all too often remain unworn, consigned almost immediately to the back of the wardrobe.

Even if we could change our purchasing habits, the repercussions would be great. For better and for worse, many of the world's poorest communities now depend on our purchases for their wages. The global clothing industry employs some twenty-six million people and underpins local economies and individual incomes around the world.

HOW TO REVERSE THEN WHAT SEEMS TO BE A TOTAL DISREGARD FOR THE RESOURCES, BOTH HUMAN AND ENVIRONMENTAL, THAT OUR CLOTHES REQUIRE?

In my mind, our greatest crime is not the buying itself but the carelessness with which we yield our purchasing power. In recent years, our love of consumption has fed a huge increase in clothing sales across the world. But while the British, for example, are buying a third more clothes now than they did four years ago, the amount spent per person has remained roughly the same. That means *more* is being bought for *less* – a sure-fire formula for ever-increasing wastage and the too low wages of garment workers.

The old recommendation to spend *more* on *less* needs to be resurrected. Rejecting fast fashion in favour of 'investment pieces' will keep workers around the world employed while still indulging our acquisitive instincts.

# A UNIFORM APPROACH

**25** The biologist E. O. Wilson argues in his book *The Social Conquest of Earth* that the human instinct to form groups or tribes and to defend them at all costs has been key to our development. He points out that while much has been written about the selfish gene, more focus should be placed on how our predisposition for collective behaviour has contributed to human development.

Sartorially, it seems to me that the uniform best represents our biological urge to blend into the pack, work together as one of the team or declare our affiliation with a community, company or profession. A uniform can be a formal requirement, such as a school, military or police uniform, but equally it can be the product of social conventions, a quasi-uniform such as those worn by the businessperson, football fan or clubber.

To some extent, all of us are wearing a uniform of one form or another every time we leave home because the clothes we choose to wear speak volumes about our allegiance to a social tribe. Societal norms determine that we make our image chime with current expectations. If we do not dress appropriately, we cannot build a career or have much of a social life. From work to special occasions, we have to dress the part.

Naturally, some of us love to subvert expectations and challenge conventions. Every generation has its own subcultures that rebel against current notions of respectability. But think about it: what are the looks cultivated by the Mods of the 1960s, Punks of the late 1970s or the all-black Goths of the 1980s but uniforms that identified their wearers' allegiance to a particular tribe?

# BEYOND THE BOTTOM LINE

**26** The Internet, globalization and an increasingly culturally amalgamated world mean that, if we so choose, we can all now easily buy goods and services that embody our values from a variety of international sources. Where, why and how we choose to buy our clothes has become a reflection of who we are, and as consumers we are ever more keen to explore and express our individuality through our purchases.

Fashion designers should take note. Competition in today's complex and interconnected fashion industry is fierce and standing out in a crowded market difficult. To compete, designers must capture the aesthetic imagination of the individual and meet the expectations of a sophisticated global audience.

> The key is to keep the consumer always in mind even as you, the designer, bring your own values to the fore. Continue to design clothes that epitomize great design and use high-quality materials, but do think twice before ignoring issues of environmental responsibility and ethical production standards. Consumers' expectations of fashion are changing and so must the industry's. Adapting will be a challenge, a daunting and even overwhelming one, but the designer that puts his or her values first, and the bottom line second, will stand out from the crowd.

Think of Stella McCartney, who has always insisted on putting her beliefs at the heart of the design process. Her clothes are desirable, beautiful and produced in such a way as not to compromise her values. As she explains: 'Everything in my store and every single garment and accessory that you see is cruelty-free, in the sense that no animal has died to make anything in here. A lot of people out there don't want products that an animal has had to die for.' McCartney's customers buy her clothes primarily for their great design, but there is also no doubt that her commitment to her own ethics sets her and her label apart.

> Yuniya Kawamura, a professor at the Fashion Institute of Technology in New York, writes: 'Fashion may be socially frivolous but it is not sociologically trivial.' The designers who understand this wisdom and integrate it into their design processes will have the greatest impact today.

# EVERY WEEK IS FASHION WEEK

**27** Every year, over two hundred fashion weeks occur across the world. It is not just London, Milan, Paris and New York hosting these events dedicated to displaying the latest thinking in fashion. From Sydney to Lagos, Mumbai to Shanghai, Rio de Janeiro to Kiev, the creative, economic and dynamic force that is fashion is displayed and celebrated. Some nations even have two cities rivalling each other for fashion domination, as in China and India.

There is an ongoing debate about whether or not blogging, tweeting, live-streaming and other media are going to bring about the demise of the traditional fashion-week format, with its catwalk shows, buying events, parties and photo shoots. The argument goes that it is all becoming too expensive for journalists, buyers and fashionistas to keep attending the ever-increasing number of showcases.

I don't believe the days of the fashion week are numbered. Rather their growth demonstrates the economic power of the fashion industry and its relevance to communities around the world. Hosting a fashion week injects a city with a certain cultural cachet and kudos; it's a statement that it too should hold a notable position on the aesthetic world stage. It also satisfies our very real need to have glamour, performance and fun in our lives. Every nation and every ambitious city wants the spectacle and cachet that a fashion week brings.

# TRENDSETTER, TRENDSHIRKER

**28** If you type the words 'philosophy' and 'fashion' into Google, the search engine will inform you that 'About 68,400,000 results' have been located in '0.12 seconds'. Reading through all these results might take a million years in itself, but a cursory run through some of the earliest links quickly reveals a unifying instructional emphasis: how we as individuals can develop and evolve a uniquely personal approach to dress, or, in other words, our own philosophy of fashion.

CLOTHES SAY SOMETHING TO THE WORLD ABOUT WHO YOU ARE; THEY ARE VISUAL INDICATORS OF THE PRIVATE DECISIONS WE MAKE EVERY MORNING WHEN WE CHOOSE WHAT TO WEAR FOR THE DAY.

On the symbolic power of clothes, art historian Quentin Bell has written, 'Our clothes are too much a part of us for most of us ever to be entirely indifferent to their condition: it is as though the fabric were indeed a natural extension of the body, or even the soul.' That clothes touch us both emotionally and physically has preoccupied many academics, theorists and philosophers. As Roland Barthes, the theorist and author of *The Fashion System*, wrote: 'Clothing concerns all of the human person, all of the body, all of the relationships of man to body as well as the relationships of the body to society.' Dressing oneself, Barthes argued, is a highly personal act through which we, as individuals, select and don the clothes that reflect the social group to which we belong or aspire to belong. 'The wearing of an item of clothing is fundamentally an act of meaning that goes beyond modesty, ornamentation and protection. It is an act of signification and therefore a profoundly social act right at the heart of the dialectic of society.'

It seems perfectly understandable to me why so many people are interested in cultivating their own fashion philosophy, the rationale being that the clothes you wear and the way you wear them silently communicate something of your inner self to friends, peers and strangers. Developing your own philosophy of fashion also frees you from the industry's trends, arbiters of taste and seasonal changes. Which is not to say that you should never again check out the latest catwalk shows or flip through your favourite fashion magazine. By all means still take inspiration or insight from the fashion world. I suspect though that with a fashion philosophy, you will feel less pressured to wear an item of clothing no matter how unflattering or uncomfortable it may be. Leather trousers, platform shoes, sleeveless dresses – these are just a few of the things that don't make the cut in my own (ever-evolving) philosophy of fashion.

# COVER UP

**29** Around the world, in countries both developed and developing, how women dress is still a contentious issue. Whether in Egypt, India, South Africa, Mexico, the United States, France or the United Kingdom, discussions about what is the most 'suitable' way for a woman to dress continue.

Too much skin showing? Too little? Societal expectations vary culture to culture but depressingly, even in the so-called liberated

West, you can always find justifications of verbal, physical and sexual assaults based on how the female victim was dressed at the time. The SlutWalk protest marches that began in Toronto in 2011 started as a response to a police officer's comment that 'women should avoid dressing like sluts in order not to be victimized'.

Let's be clear. Provocative dress is not a provocation. Clothes should be about allowing and empowering a woman's self-expression, rather than defining who she is or what she wants. I do believe though that the power of clothing is too often underestimated. How you dress will always affect how people respond to you. It's inevitable. But a justification for assault? Never.

# PERFECTING OUR LIFE/STYLE

**30** If fashion is now ubiquitous, global in its reach and spread, and central to how individuals express themselves, what is behind its power? Is it the clothes, the make-up, the accessories? Or did the American anthropologist Ted Polhemus get it right when in 2005 he wrote: 'At the heart of lifestyle is style – today's vital, indispensable language of identity. From an ever-growing supermarket of style . . . we choose those items which signify most precisely where we are "at".'

# 31

# FACT: WATER

Fashion is a super consumer of water, which is used at almost every stage of the industry's highly complex supply chain. From growing the raw materials to the dyeing and processing of fabrics, from manufacturing the garments to transporting them to market, at every stage large quantities of water are consumed. IT TAKES 2,700 LITRES OF WATER TO PRODUCE ONE COTTON T-SHIRT FROM 'CROP TO SHOP'. Imagine how many swimming pools of water it took to manufacture the contents of your wardrobe – and how many more swimming pools will go into extending its lifespan through regular washes at home. In the meantime, five thousand children die each day due to a lack of clean water. Dwindling cotton yields, rising water scarcity and the increasing number of droughts worldwide means that that number may soon be increasing. The fashion industry must rethink the way it consumes water *now*.

# A MOLECULAR TREND

**32** Let's take a moment to view fashion through a different lens. It was Professor Juan Hinestroza of the Textiles Nanotechnology Laboratory at Cornell University who first opened my eyes to fashion at a molecular level: 'Fashion designers see garments as an expression of creativity. Chemists and material scientists see garments as a collection of molecules. Now we can take these molecules and create fashion with function.' Could understanding a garment as an arrangement of molecules that lives on once we are finished with it be the key to recognizing and addressing the long-term environmental consequences of fashion?

# DRESS UP TO DRESS DOWN

**33** Dressing and undressing are intensely private experiences. Central to both acts are the garments themselves, the underwear and outerwear that each morning we put on and each evening we take off. Throughout the day, our clothes continue to interact with us. We move from inside to outside and throw on a coat; we turn on the heating and take off a sweater. We think nothing of it but we are forever putting on and taking off items of clothing.

We underestimate how difficult the physical act of dressing can be. While clothes may be central to who we are, all of us at certain points in our lives have needed, and may yet need, assistance dressing and undressing ourselves. Learning to dress yourself, from putting on a T-shirt to tying your own shoelaces, is a pivotal process in becoming independent. It's a rite of passage. Choosing for the first time which clothes to buy with your own pocket money is equally a key moment in the evolving definition of who you are. In short, our clothes and the rituals surrounding the acts of putting them on or removing them have lasting value and significance to us.

# WHY *CLOTHES* MATTER

**34** If fashion matters, clothes matter too. They are our primary protection from the physical world, whether that's the harsh rays of the sun, sub-zero temperatures, treacherous terrain or even one another. Clothes may cover our nakedness and protect us from the elements but there is more to them than just that. As we all know, being naked in the wrong context is still a great taboo. Clothes give us the ability both as individuals and participants in broader society to operate on a physical level with the world around us. Mark Twain was quite right when he quipped: 'Clothes make the man. Naked people have little or no influence on society.'

Fashion answers both our biological *and* cultural needs. Professor of Bioarchaeology at Bournemouth University, Holger Schutkowski suggests that attempting to unravel which need should take precedence is futile: 'The ability of humans to create and respond to the cultured environment is a cornerstone of the dual human nature. Whether biology or culture takes precedence is almost a moot point, as the two are so intimately intertwined to the point of being inseparable.'

# DRAWING A LINE

**35** Children's clothes are a major part of the fashion industry. In 2011, this subcategory was worth $10 billion and an ever-growing number of blogs and designer lines are specifically targeted at children. Significant sums are being spent: $60 for a T-shirt; $500 for a jacket. Direct spending by teenagers and children has tripled since 1990. As fashion and popular culture have become synonymous, younger consumers are being exposed to fashion at a younger and younger age. Advertising campaigns directed at children put enormous pressure on parents who have neither the money nor the desire to dress children in this way. As a fashion enthusiast, even I am wary of the new phenomenon that is London's Global Kids Fashion Week.

How in our commercial, image-driven world can we tread a line between great children's clothes that are attractive, well made and beautifully designed without exploiting children and encouraging an unhealthy focus on the superficial, body image and price tag? Children are far more susceptible to outside influences than adults yet all too often fashion campaigns for children are selling the same dreams that make adults feel inadequate, not empowered.

It is time for the fashion industry to take responsibility for how children feel about themselves. Fashion and clothing for young people should be about experimentation, not about conforming to a stereotype. We owe our children this freedom.

# THE T-SHIRT TAKEOVER

**36** The T-shirt is a favourite fashion staple. Easy to dress up or down depending on the occasion, it is the workhorse of every wardrobe and anyone under the age of seventy is bound to have at least one or two in their wardrobe.

The T-shirt's freedom of movement and swift drying ability are owed to its origins as part of the uniform of both the British Navy and the American Navy. The hosiery boom, emphasis on hygiene and the comfort of having soft cotton next to your skin to stop chaffing all contributed to the T-shirt's swift adoption across the armed forces and then more generally. In 1941 the slogan 'You don't need to be a soldier to have your own personal T-shirt' confirmed it as *the* wardrobe staple of the manly man.

The T-shirt's reputation as an item of clothing with a message – both literally in terms of printed slogans and because it was underwear now being worn as outerwear – took hold. It became a democratic symbol with everyone and anyone, women included, now wearing one, from Elvis Presley to John F. Kennedy, Brigitte Bardot to Katharine Hamnett. The development of heat transfers and screen-printing in the 1960s led to the printed T-shirt, which might feature images from surfing culture on either its front or back, or, after bands such as The Grateful Dead identified its promotional possibilities, the details of a concert tour. These days every film, show, concert, charity, school, university and company seems to use the T-shirt as a promotional tool.

Over the years, the T-shirt has lost some of its cutting-edge, sub-cultural references but it remains a potent symbol of democratic fashion and how far a garment can evolve from its origins.

# BACK TO BLACK

**37** A perennial cliché is that those at the heart of the fashion industry – the individuals promoting colourful, patterned, often experimental clothes each season – only wear black themselves. Now a quick look at any fashion coverage will disprove this as a rule, but there is an element of truth here. Black is always in fashion. Green, mustard, pink, orange, even navy, grey, white and camel, these colours appear, disappear and then reappear on the catwalks over the years, but black remains a constant.

Black is a powerful colour with many cultural associations. Dressing all in black is often a sophisticated, elegant and restrained fashion statement, yet even so the historical associations of black with evil, death, eroticism, piety and Puritanism remain. In the past, black was predominantly worn by mourners grieving the death of a loved one, though poets, priests, artists and intellectuals also donned the sombre colour to set themselves apart. Black denoted wealth too as the dye required to create it was very expensive. Only in Victorian times were cheaper dyes developed.

Despite all that exuberant colours have to offer, designers such as Donna Karan, Yves Saint Laurent, Yohji Yamamoto, Comme des Garçons and Ann Demeulemeester return to black again and again. Timeless and classic, the favourite colour of Coco Chanel and Audrey Hepburn, black focuses the eye on the fabric, silhouette and texture of a garment. It flatters the figure and can be worn anywhere with anything.

# FOR THE LOVE OF A LABEL

**38** Why are people prepared to pay so much more for an item of clothing or an accessory simply because of its label? For me, the twentieth-century French artist Marcel Duchamp shed more light on this question than any fashion commentator. It was 1917 when he infamously scrawled the signature 'R. Mutt' on the side of an upturned urinal, titled it *Fountain* and submitted it for exhibition as a work of art. Duchamp believed that in labelling the urinal art, it *became* art. *Fountain* was summarily rejected by the exhibition curators, but Duchamp's theory that we value objects primarily because of their label rather than for their purpose became famous.

Duchamp is widely lauded for revolutionizing how we view and understand art. His observations, such as 'Living is more a question of what one spends than what one makes,' and 'Art is either

plagiarism or revolution,' are equally applicable to fashion. But why
do we value the label or logo of an object more than the object itself?

In fashion, as elsewhere, this skewed assigning of value is about
authority and recognition; the authority of the person or brand
behind the label and the recognition of people who know what that
brand represents. And so we sometimes enter the fairy-tale world of
The Emperor's New Clothes when just because we are told something is fashionable and worth more, we believe it to be so.

# MEN IN HIGH-HEELS

**39** High-heels arrived in Europe in 1599 with the diplomatic visit of the
Persian royal court. In Persia, high-heeled shoes had developed in
order to enable riders to stand up in their stirrups when fighting on
horseback. In Europe, they would fast become a symbol of wealth,
power – and masculinity.

High-heels on the streets of seventeenth-century Europe were
useless but that was the point. If you were wearing them you had
to be wealthy, privileged and high born. During Louis XIV's reign,
red high-heels became a feature of royal dress and an indication of
whether or not you were in favour. Red high-heels meant you were
in. Any other colour – social outcast.

# THE WORLD NEEDS MORE WINTOUR

**40** Why is it that in fashion, an industry predominantly devoted to making and meeting the desires of women, so few women rise to the top? While there are growing numbers of women in senior, high-profile positions, from Anna Wintour and Stella McCartney to Natalie Massenet and Jane Sheperdson, nevertheless in the United Kingdom, where fifty-two per cent of women account for the workforce, only thirty-seven per cent hold senior positions. These statistics are replicated the world over. They may be better than in many industries but they are still not good enough.

There are signs of improvement. Increasing numbers of clothing and accessory manufacturers are removing discriminatory practices that prevented or deterred women from undertaking what were considered to be men's jobs. In emerging economies, more women are founding start-ups and co-operatives with truly significant knock-on effects to family planning and female education, which in turn improve the health and well-being of women and children. Women are behind many of the online fashion businesses that exist today, precisely because their founders were looking to balance work around family life. Established businesses need to work harder to provide similar flexibility. The future of the fashion industry holds real opportunities for greater equality, diversity and achievements, something that would benefit all consumers and producers, men and women.

# 41

# A QUESTION OF EXPOSURE

Do we wear clothes to cover our nakedness and fashion to suggest our nudity?

# NOT JUST ANOTHER BRANDING TOOL

**42** What does it mean for something to be 'in fashion'? Is it just another way to say that something is fashionable?

At the Shanghai International Fashion Forum in 2013, I was struck by how many global businesses and industries, from architecture through to exhibition design, were actively seeking to transform their products from basic commodities into luxury items, using fashion as the catalyst. Fashion, to them, was simply a branding tool with which to reposition their companies and their products as fashionable.

If everything is now fashion-driven and every sector want to be 'in fashion', where does that leave actual fashion? Surely not everything can be 'in fashion' – that would be a contradiction of terms.

# FASHIONING STEREOTYPES

**43** In her book *Fashion and Celebrity Culture*, Pamela Church Gibson discusses the sexualization of the female image and the lengths that women will go to achieve this ideal. Church Gibson distinguishes between the angular, slim, tall young woman of the catwalk, favoured by 'devotees of high fashion', and the more prevalent and acceptable ideal of 'contemporary glamour': the 'toned-down porn star' with her fake hair, breasts, lips, nails and skin tone. Each ideal is damaging in its own way but the heady sexualization of the latter is particularly detrimental to the education, ambitions and self-confidence of girls and women because it suggests that sexual desirability is the only measure of a woman's value in society.

Recent research from the United States that examined differences between white and black women's views of their bodies concluded that because black women encounter fewer representations of black women in the media, they have a more positive view of themselves than white women. So while we must encourage the better representation of all races, we should be clear that not all forms of representation are equally desirable. Some are clearly damaging. We must fight back and demand that idealized and constructed images of women are not the only ones encountered in the world of fashion and beyond.

# THE CREATIVE CONSUMER

**44** The Internet and social media have profoundly altered the relationship between creators and consumers. It reminds me of a quote from the Canadian philosopher Marshall McLuhan: 'The wheel is the extension of the foot; the book is an extension of the eye; clothing, an extension of the skin; electric circuitry, an extension of the central nervous system.' Written in the early 1960s, McLuhan's point that technologies improve and extend human capabilities foreshadowed the rise of the Internet and our era of near instant communication. The Internet acts as an extension of our brains, linking us one to another across the world like so many neural highways. Air travel brought humans closer; the Internet linked our brains.

We live in a time when if we want to know something, we can learn about it almost instantaneously. When if we see something and want it, we can order it up online and have it delivered the next day. The Internet has changed not only how we access knowledge and objects but also how designers, retailers and consumers interact.

Fashion was quick to catch on to the possibilities. In 2002 Japanese fashion designer Yohji Yamamoto produced a pattern for Nick Knight's SHOWstudio website that empowered anybody to download it, make up the garment and then post an image of themselves wearing it. The design remained Yamamoto's, but the material and way it was styled and recorded was down to each consumer. More recently, beyond the world of fashion, similar consumer involvement resulted in the 2011 film *Life in a Day*. Here, people were invited to record an hour of their lives and submit it to the film's producers and director. So successful was this crowd-sourcing initiative that some eighty thousand clips were uploaded to YouTube, far exceeding expectations for the number of submissions. The edited film may be the work of its commissioners but the people own the content.

The line between the producer and the consumer is becoming ever more blurred. Blogs such as The Man Repeller and Garance Doré, which started out as the personal projects of their founders, went on to develop cult followings and now sell advertising and have become involved in retailing and the development of a whole new brand. Online shopping makes possible mass customization so anyone can design and tailor their footwear or clothing exactly to their own requirements or desires, including the colour, pattern or fit.

> NEW TECHNOLOGIES ARE GOING TO CHANGE THINGS YET AGAIN. THE TIME IS FAST APPROACHING WHEN WE WILL ALL BE ABLE TO BUY 3D PRINTERS, ADDING THEM TO THE SCANNERS, CAMERAS AND DIGITAL PRINTERS WE ALREADY OWN. AT THIS POINT, ANYONE WITH AN IDEA WILL BE ABLE TO DESIGN, MANUFACTURE AND SELL A PRODUCT.

In this new economy, what will be the roles of the designer and traditional manufacturer? Who will be the producer and who will make what for whom? How might the rise of creative consumers transform the fashion industry? Will it be in their own image?

# THE BRA AS FASHION STAPLE

**45** Many Western consumers donate their unwanted garments to charity shops, which sift and sort the garments, keeping some to sell and exporting others to the developing world. This reuse of clothing is beneficial from an environmental perspective but can have negative effects on the development of the local economies that receive these imports. While local market traders might make a profit from selling this foreign product, the local textile and garment-making industries struggle to compete and the development of a robust skilled workforce – and the higher wages that go with it – stalls.

A number of major charities and NGOs are working to diminish these economic repercussions and ensure that local markets and domestic textile and garment producers are nurtured rather than hindered by Western donations. One particularly interesting example involves Oxfam and the humble – or not, as the case may be – bra.

> Most women will admit that at least a couple of unworn and unwanted bras hide away in the dark recesses of their wardrobes. That neon number that seemed a good idea at the time; that practical beige one you replaced two years ago but never threw out; that gift from an ex-boyfriend – we all have them. Rarely do these bras make their way to charity shops, however, because most women believe there is no market for second-hand underwear. This is incorrect. Used bras are actually very much in demand in Africa, particularly in Senegal, and Oxfam has launched a campaign to encourage donations.

Constructing and manufacturing bras is a complex process and difficult to replicate without access to the latest factory technologies. For this reason, bras donated from the developed world do not put local makers out of business because there *are* no local makers – of bras, that is. There are, of course, plenty of skilled makers, and in Senegal it's these entrepreneurs who have created a whole new cottage industry repairing, or 'up-cycling', bras into desirable and fashionable products, which they can then sell in markets at prices generating profits of up to fifty per cent. Senegalese women are keen to buy these bras not only for the comfort and dignity they provide but also as a stylish accessory. Frequently worn over top of other clothes, the bra has become a fashion staple.

# TECHNOLOGICAL TENACITY

**46** If you were to look in your wardrobe and consider what was the most important technological innovation in your clothes, what would it be? We tend to think of technology in terms of computers and other electronic devices, but many technologies are very simple in concept. Perhaps, it would be the simple button or the hook and eye or maybe even a pocket? Would it be Lycra, the first commercial polyester fibre developed by DuPont in 1954? The first sewing machine, patented in the United States in 1842? Or would it be the zip, which was developed in 1913 and has revolutionized our clothes and our accessories. If you had to, what would you choose?

# A SEAT ON THE FRONT ROW

**47** In an age of online shopping, instant messaging, blogs and social media, the catwalk show has remained at the heart of fashion. Rather than consigning the twenty-minute spectacle to history, designers and brands have instead embraced its inherent theatricality as never before, using Twitter and live-streaming to make every customer feel they have a front-row seat. Backstage posts and Tweets capturing the behind-the-scenes antics of models, stylists, commentators and photographers preparing for the show help to raise the tempo and build anticipation even before the clothes hit the runway. Panel discussions, extensive media coverage and amateur and professional commentators alike keep the discussion going, ensuring that the show, and therefore the clothes, remains a topic of discussion long after the last model has exited the stage.

Over the past two decades, the fashion show has transformed from its static 'fashion parade' origins into a multimedia, multi-sensory performance. French creative mastermind Alexandre de Betak is partly responsible for this transition; his fashion shows, installations, events and exhibits for a range of clients, from Dior to H&M, are extraordinary, lavish affairs. In a 2013 interview with the Business of Fashion, de Betak commented on the role of the fashion show today: 'Now that the means of communication are worldwide and immediate, I think people are tired of seeing too much of the same. . . . I think today consumers want to be surprised, they want more individualism, more right angles, more weird decisions taken. Of course, brands still need to be recognizable for who they are, but I think more and more they also need to be surprising and reinvent themselves.'

Often the staging of the fashion show outshines the garments on display. In July 2013, Chanel staged its autumn/winter haute couture show within what appeared to be a bombed-out theatre, built to scale within Paris's cavernous Grand Palais. This set had more column inches devoted to it than the clothes did, but that was the point. In a world where novelty and innovation is key, this controversial production made Chanel a talking point. British fashion house Burberry has innovated by taking a different tack: consumers watching its live-streamed fashion shows online can, from anywhere in the world, order the garments coming down the catwalk then and there. Digital access to the fashion show has not diminished the exclusivity of the event itself. If anything, it has only reinforced the air of elitism and glamour that has always given fashion its unique cultural cachet.

# THE OPTICALLY ENHANCED WHITE SHIRT

**48** One of the most versatile items of clothing in a woman's wardrobe is the white shirt. Crisp and fresh, signalling strength and independence (perhaps because of its history as a men's clothing staple), it looks appropriate in any situation: at the Oscars worn by Sharon Stone, on a Patti Smith album cover, worn to a business meeting with a suit, or paired with jeans at a concert. The white shirt is versatile, democratic, androgynous and feminine. It is a staple of every wardrobe. What we don't recognize is the price we pay for its appealing absence of colour.

White fabrics, often associated with cleanliness, even godliness, rely on optical brighteners for their even whiteness. Optical brighteners are made using stilbenes, one of the most widely used chemical groups in the manufacture of paper, detergents and textiles. Stilbenes reflect light and are applied to fabrics after bleaching to make them look brighter than they actually are. Stilbenes are also toxic to fish and can cause allergies when in contact with skin that has been exposed to the sun. The detergents that help keep a shirt white over its lifetime by softening water and helping to disperse dirt contain thirty per cent phosphates, which when flushed into wastewater encourage the growth of green algae that chokes other water-based organisms. A well-pressed white shirt might symbolize perfection for many women but the environment pays a high price as a result.

# INDIAN INITIATIVE

**49** In 2012 I travelled to Jaipur, India, for the annual conference of the International Federation for Fashion Technology Institutes. That year the theme was Fashion Beyond Borders and speakers and delegates had been invited to look at the roles technology, globalization and craft play in the fashion industry and the resulting implications for educational institutions around the world.

In his keynote speech, Rajeev Sethi challenged us to find ways of balancing high and low technologies. As Chairman of the Asian Heritage Foundation and a leading designer, Sethi has made it his mission to bring contemporary relevance to the time-honoured skills of South Asian artisans. He explained that India is an entrepreneurial country with a wide range of skills and knowledge, but while modernization and globalization are empowering many individuals through improved access to education and higher standards of living, they are also edging out traditional businesses and pushing highly skilled craftspeople from self-reliance to dependence. How can the exquisite hand-weaving of this country compete on price with the cheap industrial fabrics off-loaded from both foreign and domestic textile mills?

Sethi backs and lobbies for initiatives that help artisans to maintain their livelihoods. He is quick to note that these initiatives are not attempts to withstand advances in technology or to hold back industrialization but rather empower traditional producers to develop self-sustaining creative industries that can thrive now and in the future. Indian fashion designers such as Manish Aurora and Abraham and Thakore are embracing traditional skills in the design of garments that often fuse Western cuts with Indian fabrics, surface decoration and detailing – and which look as fashionable on the streets of Paris as in Mumbai.

Sethi pointed out that 'Westernization is not modernization.' Modern India will be most successful if it puts its past at the heart of its future.

# FASHION SIGNATURES

**50** Inevitably, we are all products of our childhood, family, education and cultural heritage. At the London College of Fashion, where we have students attending from over one hundred countries, it is fascinating to see how national identity manifests itself in the collections. Every year, fashion design students set out to develop their own signatures. The most successful draw on and integrate their life experiences and backgrounds into the design process, forging a unique voice in the process.

# FASHION AND
# FEMINISM

**51** Djurdja Bartlett, an expert on Soviet fashion, has written how 'following the 1917 Bolshevik revolution, . . . one of Lenin's closest collaborators, Alexandra Kollontai, was shunned by her comrades because of her good looks, her smart dresses and her sexually liberated views.' Bartlett continues on to remark, 'This made me wonder, once again, why the Left historically has had such a hostile relationship to fashion?'

It is a question I often consider myself, particularly since we *still* wrestle with the legacy of such prejudices, which are not just the preserve of the Left. For most people, to be politically engaged means not showing an overt interest in fashion.

I AM A FEMINIST AND A FASHION ENTHUSIAST. For some, this statement just can't be true for being a feminist means avoiding all things feminine and fashionable in order to demonstrate a commitment to the cause. Fashion is frivolous and fun, their logic seems to be, and feminism is neither. But I see no contradiction. Politics, intellectual engagement and fashion are not mutually exclusive, whatever side of the political spectrum you fall on.

# 52

# FACT:
# THE
# ONE-
# TRILLION-
# DOLLAR
# INDUSTRY

The fashion industry is hugely important economically. It is worth over $1 trillion globally and ranked the second biggest worldwide economic activity for intensity of trade.

# A SHORT HISTORY OF FACIAL HAIR

**53** In 1993 the artist and activist David McDiarmid wrote and performed the short essay 'A Short History of Facial Hair', which was accompanied by 35 mm colour slides. A funny, hard-hitting and uncompromising piece, it charted a twenty-year period of his own life, during which he went from hippy to sexual revolutionary to HIV-positive queer subject, and powerfully demonstrated how gay politics changed during what he described as 'an extraordinary time of redefinition and deconstruction of our identities from camp to gay to queer'. By charting his personal fashion choices, hair and facial hair, McDiarmid told the story of his life in a time of changing political and sexual mores.

If ever an artwork made the link between art, identity, politics, dress and adornment, this was it.

# THE LUXURY/ FASHION FACE-OFF

**54** 'Luxury' has become a fashionable word and so-called luxury brands are keen to exploit our desire for high-quality and prestigious goods. Yet the relationship between fashion and luxury is not an easy one.

Luxury goods have traditionally stood for all that is timeless, finely crafted and beautiful, with their expense and rarity adding to their exclusivity. Fashion, on the other hand, is about constant change and reinvention. It taps into our love of the new.

This apparent contradiction breaks down at the top end of the market because the hefty price tags attached to luxury goods do not dissuade the world's wealthiest from refreshing their wardrobe and accessories with new purchases every season. A shopping spree at Chanel or Harrods is for them the same as a spree at Gap would be for us.

Still, luxury brands recognize that while the vast majority of consumers cannot afford their sky-high prices, they want a piece of the luxury dream advertised in glitzy ad campaigns. For this reason perfume, accessory and cosmetics ranges have long been more lucrative than a fashion house's core clothing offer. That split is widening further. Couture remains a loss leader underpinned by a fashion house's marketing budget, and British journalist Suzy Menkes recently predicted ready-to-wear would go the same way, that like couture it would become primarily 'a laboratory of ideas'.

With many of the skilled workers that specialize in making luxury items now residing outside Europe, there is an increasing desire among consumers for honesty and openness about the manufacturing process. Customers expect more of a luxury product than other goods and want to know how, where and in what conditions their purchases were made. There is the expectation that materials should be sourced ethically too; for example, consumers are concerned about the role of gemstones in funding war and the use of endangered animal products, such as crocodile skin, shahtoosh wool and snakeskin.

In 2007 the World Wildlife Fund report *Deeper Luxury* urged luxury brands to catch up with such expectations and to prepare for 'shifts in the luxury paradigm', stating, 'In future, the highest quality product or service will be the one that generates the most benefit to all involved in its production and trade. Consumers' knowledge of that benefit will be essential to their elite experience, and to the prestige ascribed to them by their peers.' The French luxury powerhouse Hermès is driving this trend for accountability. Its Festival des Métiers exhibition in 2013 saw the brand relocate its famous Paris workshop to London's Saatchi Gallery where visitors could watch the highly skilled artisans behind the label's iconic bags, scarves and jewelry at work. Was it all a marketing stunt? Of course. But I am hopeful that this stunt was just the beginning of an enduring change in consumer expectations. In the future, the luxury brand that cannot reassure customers of its social and environmental credentials may not be classified as a luxury brand at all.

# SKIN TO SKIN

## 55

When we first try on a garment, we are making a direct and intimate connection with the person who has made it. We are also implicitly stating that we are happy to put it next to our skins. Despite this intimate relationship, we continue to turn a blind eye to the pay and conditions of these workers.

We have little excuse: the consequences of our purchases have been drawn to our attention for years. Over a century ago, Charles Kingsley wrote in his 1870 essay, 'Cheap Clothes and Nasty', of the appalling working conditions experienced by tailors in London. Conditions may have drastically improved for the British tailor but moving the garment industry offshore has kept costs down for a reason.

Fashion should not come at any cost. Considering the efforts many of us make to look after our skin, we should take more care in ensuring the happiness of those humans whose skin first touched the clothes we wear.

# CRAFT, CREATIVITY AND COMMERCE

**56** Craft, the skilful making of something by hand, is undergoing a renaissance in the fashion industry. At the highest levels, the renowned Paris ateliers continue to create haute couture featuring exquisitely executed embroidery, beadwork and other handiwork, as they have been doing since the nineteenth century. Consumers unable to afford haute couture are disillusioned and frustrated with the exploitative practices that accompany mass manufacturing and keen to learn more about these processes. Crucially, they are also willing to pay more for handcrafted goods that identify and even promote the individuals responsible for their creation.

The fashion industry is beginning to realize that re-establishing the connection between creator and consumer has commercial as well as ethical and environmental benefits. In a particularly high-profile collaboration, TopShop partnered with the Ghanaian women's co-operative Global Mamas to launch a collection of dresses that employed traditional craft skills and ensured a sustainable income for women in Ghana. Similarly, TABEISA (Technical and Business Education Initiative in South Africa), a consortium of four South African and two British institutions, connects local makers with British retailers through their Design 4 Life competition.

Artisans in the developed world are also benefiting from the renewed interest in craft, and websites such as Etsy.com, 'the world's most vibrant handmade marketplace', allow them to bypass traditional retailers and sell direct. The global recession was in part to thank for the renewed interest in handcrafted clothes and accessories. In times of uncertainty we often choose to take comfort in tradition, and knitting groups and sewing circles have become more mainstream.

For the vast majority of human history, craft was integral to cultural expression and the creation of our clothes. Inuit beadwork, Peruvian embroidery, African kente textiles, Harris tweed, Kashmiri shawls and Japanese silks are all examples of craft, and by extension human ingenuity and dexterity. Until the Industrial Revolution, garments were constructed by hand, through knitting, crochet, needlework, dyeing, weaving, embroidery and leather tooling. The cultivation of new crafts and the resurrection of the old rightly return the emphasis in fashion to human skills and the people responsible for our clothes.

# FRESH-FACED
# TO THE WORLD

**57** School biology classes teach us that skin is our largest organ. The multiple layers of the ectoderm guard our internal organs, muscles and skeletal structure, and hold us together while simultaneously protecting us from the external environment, be that pathogens and bacteria, the sun or the weather. It is easy to forget how fine this layer is, between two and three millimetres, and only when we cut or burn ourselves, or pop a blister after wearing an uncomfortable pair of shoes, do we remember.

Skin is a key part of how we view and define beauty. Fresh, smooth, unlined, plump and even in tone – that is how our skin is meant to look. We are under great pressure to ensure that our skin conforms to this notion of beauty, whatever our age, gender or ethnicity.

If you were to ask people what affects their self-confidence the most, how their skin looks and feels would be high on the list. We all know how embarrassing it is facing other people when our skin has broken out in spots or blemishes, a rash or eczema. Our skin communicates something of our internal state of mind; others assess not only our attractiveness but also our mood and health from its condition. From Botox to skin whiteners, skin peels to fillers, women and men across the world, from all cultures and of all ethnicities, go to great lengths and expense to make their skin as 'perfect' as possible.

A study undertaken by Proctor & Gamble skincare scientist Paul Matts discovered that even the actual logistics of human vision affect how we view others. Our eyes rely on contrast to perceive the world;

without it, we would essentially be blind. This means our vision is biologically attuned to notice the development of wrinkles, furrows, unevenness in skin tone and other signs of ageing. Pair this genetic capability with the constant media emphasis on the young and youthful and a steady rise in cosmetic surgery has been the result.

The colour and age of our skin should not define us. Being comfortable in your own skin should not necessitate medical procedures that try to turn back the clock. Instead, let's mimic snakes and at each stage of our lives metaphorically shed our skins, renewing ourselves by embracing, not ridiculing, how we look at this new point in our lives.

# THE CHANGING ROOM

**58** One of the most striking phenomena of the past decade has been the growth in online retail. Books, music, DVDs, basic foodstuffs and white goods make up the majority of online shopping transactions and that makes sense – you can get a good feel for these things without having to touch them. Fashion on the other hand is usually tried on prior to purchase, so the exponential growth of online fashion retail in recent years took many by surprise. Not me though.

To me it makes perfect sense and it is all down to changing rooms. Whether it's an overheated communal changing room, a cubical so small that you can barely turn around let alone bend over or harsh neon lighting and a mirror jointly committed to showing your body in the most unflattering light, the changing room always manages to do its worst. The result? An immediate loss of confidence, a wave of flustered irritability and the irrational belief that your less than perfect body is truly unforgivable.

If there were only some way to try on clothes without having to get naked first, that would help, for there is something inherently undermining in undressing in a changing room. Somehow the freedom associated with the semi-nudity we enjoy when swimming, on holiday or at the gym evaporates. The pressure to determine whether the clothes do or do not somehow project the person we feel ourselves to be doesn't help – nor does the unsympathetic eye of the sales assistant.

## SHOPPING IN STORE CAN BE A PLEASURABLE EXPERIENCE IN MANY WAYS THAT ONLINE SHOPPING CANNOT RIVAL.

I myself love a day at the shops exploring floors, investigating the rails, touching and feeling the different textures and materials. Yet online shopping offers the opportunity to avoid a changing room and for that more and more shoppers are embracing it. Order up the latest fashions and try them on in the privacy of one's own home? Yes, please. Safe from prying eyes, there the self-conscious shopper can take his or her time when deciding whether or not to keep the new garment and even try it on with other items in the wardrobe. The best retail sites make returning any unwanted goods both easy and free so really the risks are few, the rewards great.

# THE GOLDEN GOOSE

**59** The suicide of Alexander McQueen and the drug and alcohol addictions that precipitated John Galliano's fall from grace have led to speculation that not only is the fashion industry content to damage the environment and exploit garment workers, but it also puts undue pressures on the designers themselves. That was the tack at least that Galliano took in the court proceedings that followed his anti-Semitic and racist rants of 2011.

Regardless of the particulars of Galliano's case, it is certainly true that the fashion designer is responsible for more than ever before. The annual fashion cycle traditionally meant two couture collections per year: spring/summer and autumn/winter. Biannual ready-to-wear collections followed, sometimes replacing couture but not always. Today many of the leading fashion houses have added to these four collections two inter-season collections, a pre-season collection, a resort collection and a diffusion line, not to mention accessories and jewelry.

Big-name fashion designers have a lot of help and are well compensated for their creative output, so I am not suggesting that we feel sorry for them or band together to protect their rights. But it does bear pointing out that creativity and commercial imperatives might not make for the best of bedmates.

I find two quotes particularly insightful in their weighing up of the challenges that come with commercial creativity. The first comes from Rei Kawakubo, the seminal designer behind Comme des Garçons, in an interview with *Women's Wear Daily*: 'The motivation has always been to create something new, something that didn't exist before. The more experience I have and the more clothes I make, the more difficult it becomes to make something new. Once I've made something, I don't want to do it again, so the breadth of possibility is becoming smaller.'

The designer Azzedine Alaïa spoke to the Business of Fashion website about industry attempts to rationalize and schedule a designer's creative process and his resistance to this corporate approach: 'I refuse to work in a static rhythm. Why should I sacrifice my creativity to that? That's not fashion, that's industrial work. We can hire people to design all day long and then fabricate what they design and sell and sell and sell – but that has nothing to do with fashion, with *la mode*. And it's a shame talents are being abused for this. I really don't understand that.'

The fashion industry needs to be careful about how it cultivates, nurtures and sustains creative talent; stretching an individual's creativity beyond what is humanly possible risks killing the goose that lays the golden egg.

# THE ELEPHANT
# IN THE ROOM

**60** One of the biggest challenges to developing an environmentally friendly and sustainable garment industry is the end of life or
de-manufacture of clothes. It is the elephant in the room that no one
wants to discuss. The solutions are known but are rarely applied sys-
tematically or in a manner that consumers can readily understand
and implement. We may think that taking our clothes to charity
shops or giving them to friends fulfils the mantra 'reduce, reuse,
recycle' but in reality passing on our clothes for further use is only
one stop in a journey that still ends in a landfill.

Manufacturers and retailers can do more and we, as consumers, need
to insist that they do. We should ask for a network of easily accessible
collection facilities so that clothes we cannot take elsewhere can be
reused and resold in the second-hand or vintage market. We should
be able to return our clothes to where we bought them for recycling.
Retailers should be required to produce facilities for recycling and
other end-of-life solutions. These initiatives could form part of their
marketing campaigns. The fabrics and fibres of clothes that are no
longer going to be worn could be recycled into alternative products
or made into insulation and rags.

The fashion industry should be looking at other methods of fibre
construction so that even man-made fibres will become biodegradable and therefore part of a cradle-to-cradle or closed-loop solution.
We have many of the answers already but no one to insist that they
be applied. That should be our responsibility as consumers.

# JUGGLING
# A FASHION
# JUGGERNAUT

**61** To survive and grow, high-end fashion labels need both customers who buy full-price goods regularly and customers who only ever buy garments or accessories at a discount. Balancing the needs of these two groups, however, is similar to a complex and sophisticated juggling act. Set the discount too low and you lose out on much-needed sales. Set the discount too high and you risk eroding the brand's reputation. Louis Vuitton, for one, protects its image by never selling its goods at a discount. Wait for a sale on their famous monogrammed bags and you could well be waiting forever.

## JUGGLING SHORT-TERM INCREASES IN INCOME STREAMS WITH LONG-TERM IMAGE MANAGEMENT AND THE RETENTION OF TRADITIONAL CONSUMERS IS DIFFICULT.

British label Burberry became a victim of its own success in the United Kingdom when its iconic check pattern became hugely popular in the early 2000s with the 'wrong type' of clientele. Widespread counterfeiting of Burberry products further diluted the exclusivity that had made the luxury label so desirable in the first place and sales slumped. Burberry responded by pulling the check from all but five per cent of its product and restricting licence deals to a bare minimum. The turnaround took some time but was highly effective. By 2010 Burberry was fully rehabilitated as a premier luxury brand.

The online retailing of high-end fashion was initially thought to risk a brand's exclusivity, but Natalie Massenet's Net-a-Porter.com, founded in 2000, disproved that theory. So successful has it been that fashion houses have had to expand their own online offers in response. Oscar de la Renta established an online store a number of years ago to sell smaller items; that site now sells fur coats and expensive cocktail dresses too.

# TIME TO SUIT UP

**62** Fashion is supposed to be revolutionary: each season an entirely new look, cut or colour is supposed to be the next big thing. In reality, however, fashion is much more evolutionary, with the core design and even the basic construction of an item often hundreds of years old. New trends sometimes radically alter the way we dress but usually real sartorial change requires a combination of factors to bring about its universal adoption.

Take the evolution of the businessman's uniform of suit, shirt and tie. Its component garments have changed slowly and relatively little over the centuries. Adjustments to cut, fabrics and colour have varied but the suit remains as instantly recognizable now as in the past. Innovation has arisen not from one single idea but from the steady layering of tailors' and designers' interpretations over time.

The suit, or lounge suit to use its full name, is a product of nineteenth-century England and evolved from the tuxedo, which in turn was an adaptation of the eighteenth-century morning suit. Its fine fabrics, muted colours and figure-hugging cut were taken from a number of sources: from the military, including the Russian Cossacks, came the long trousers; from horse riding, the single or double vents; and from the professions, turned-up cuffs (a necessity since removing your jacket at work was frowned on).

Of all the elements that make up the suited look, the shirt is the most basic and has barely changed since its medieval origins as a front-opening tunic with sleeves and collar. Over the centuries, it has served both as workwear and fashion garment, and while its fabrics, cut and colours have changed over time, it still continues to protect skin from heavier outer fabrics.

The necktie, the suit's key accessory, actually preceded the suit in its development and adoption. During the 1670s, the neck-cloth came to supplant the lace collar as the neckwear of choice for men. The silk and linen stocks and cravats that followed eventually transformed into the tie as we know it. Once introduced, the tie was considered essential to a man's attire and convention still holds that a man is not properly dressed without a tie to accompany his two- or three-piece suit. While creative types, artists and poets from Byron onwards have flouted and played with these social conventions, even today many hotels, restaurants, workplaces and social occasions still require, either explicitly or implicitly, that men wear a tie.

The shirt, suit and tie are internationally accepted as the conventional form of professional dress, having spread from European origins to become the accepted garments for men and women in offices around the world. Whether from TopMan, J. Crew or Hugo Boss, from a tailor in Hong Kong, Thailand or Savile Row, the well-cut suit still seems to make the man.

# 63

# A QUESTION OF NATION-HOOD

To those who deride the importance of fashion, I always ask, if clothing is so unimportant and transient, why is it so much easier to identify a nation by its national dress than by its national flag?

# CONCRETE ABSTRACTION

**64** If I was to reflect on what is unique and special about fashion, I would settle on how it transforms so many aspects of our lives, both physical and conceptual. Susan B. Kaiser and Mary Lynn Damhorst describe it well when they write in their book *Critical Linkages in Textile and Clothing Subject Matter*: 'Our work relates to the physical and social worlds; deals with the relationships among people, products and processes; and shifts continually between abstract concepts and concrete forms and issues.'

# SHOP 'TIL WE DROP

**65** Shopping is now such an integral part of our lives that many of us buy something every day. It is not so much about picking up the essentials but an enjoyable activity in its own right. A day at the shops is a frequent and anticipated part of many peoples' weekend plans.

In *The Thoughtful Dresser*, Linda Grant discusses how the onset of the Industrial Revolution in the eighteenth century transformed shopping practices. Mass production, railways, the development of urban centres and a surfeit of densely concentrated workers all contributed to the development of a new infrastructure through which to source and purchase goods.

Over two hundred years on, shopping is a habit that we can't seem to kick. In 1987 the American conceptual artist Barbara Kruger memorably re-imagined René Descartes's 'I think therefore I am' for the late twentieth century: 'I shop therefore I am.'

The turbulence that beset the financial sector in recent years had at its roots an insatiable desire for more – more risk, more money, more rewards. This approach seemed to infect not only the banking industry but also other aspects of society. Consumers cited retail therapy as an excuse to shop until they dropped and a 'Because I'm worth it' attitude prevailed. Shopping became the answer to the problem regardless of what was bought.

It was the end of the nineteenth century when Marx dubbed religion 'the opium of the people'. In our increasingly secular world, I would now replace 'religion' with 'shopping'.

# OUR CROWNING GLORY

**66** In all cultures, for men and women alike, hair is vital to our sense of self. Who hasn't looked at old photographs and laughed at their many hairstyles over the years? Baby curls, lockets of hair, hair encapsulated in funeral jewelry – we use hair to mark key passages in our life. A significant change to our hair in colour, style or length is one way that many of us signal a change in our lives, whether a divorce, new relationship or change in career. It was Coco Chanel who once said: 'A woman who cuts her hair is about to change her life.'

Hair is a central part of the fashion industry. Every fashion week, hairstyles and their relationship to the clothes make for a point of discussion. Many magazines and blogs publish exclusively about hair, and industry hair shows set their own direction for the latest styles. For centuries, hair has been big business. Just think of Marie Antoinette's many wigs. In addition to the regular cut, colour or even perm, a plethora of products, creams, oils and potions promise to keep your hair looking good.

Certain aspects of the industry are controversial, including the chemical relaxants that when used on coarse or frizzy hair can burn skin and cause hair loss. The extensions business is booming – according to IBIS World, it is worth $72 to $96 million pounds in the United Kingdom alone – but at what cost? The best hair extensions are made from human hair, which is often sourced from women who have been forced to cut and sell their hair for financial reasons or because of pressure from family members. Is our need for the perfect head of hair really worth the personal sacrifice of another woman?

# YOU ARE WHAT YOU WEAR

**67** Recently a colleague of mine at the London College of Fashion asked a group of staff to undertake a deconstruction and reading of the clothes he was wearing. He then challenged us to share our conclusions about his background, education, leisure interests, food preferences and cultural choices; really anything we thought we could decode from his hair, accessories, clothes, shoes and coat. My colleague undertakes this same exercise with new students each year in order to get them thinking about the many ways we decode and read the people we meet on a day-to-day basis and how we balance our lived experiences with the stereotypes pushed through films, TV shows, newspapers and magazines.

It is fascinating how much we think we can guess about someone from his or her appearance – and frightening how often what we guess holds true. But the exercise also revealed the risks in jumping to conclusions. Sometimes we were correct but we also got it spectacularly wrong on a few things.

It made me think how carefully I choose my clothes, accessories, hairstyle and even make-up because I think that together they say something to the world about me, about who I am. In a way, we use our clothes as a proxy for language, and as with all communication our appearance can be misunderstood. We can misread others and in our globalized world the opportunities for miscommunication are becoming even greater.

# CRISTÓBAL ON COUTURE

**68** Examining a fashion designer's perspective on his or her work can give intriguing insight into the creative process that underpins fashion. Let us pause then on the words of one of the designers I admire most, Cristóbal Balenciaga: 'A couturier must be an architect for design, a sculptor for shape, a painter for colour, a musician for harmony and a philosopher for temperance.'

# THE MEDIA
# MONOPOLY
# ON BEAUTY

**69** The fashion industry is often viewed as the main culprit in undermining women's self-esteem. Advertising campaigns, editorial shoots and catwalk shows feature only the tiniest proportion of women in society: very tall, very thin, white young women. It is not that these women are not beautiful but rather that the fashion industry perpetuates the myth that they represent the only legitimate type of beauty. Is it really all that surprising that the fashion industry has been accused of stealing a woman's love of herself only to offer it back for the price of a product?

In her 1978 anti-diet book, *Fat is a Feminist Issue*, Susie Orbach argued that female identity was inextricably linked to body image, leading to conditions such as anorexia and bulimia, just as insecurities over ageing can lead to cosmetic surgery. Orbach suggested that body hatred was a peculiarly Western export, fuelled by the media's essentially misogynist perceptions of female beauty. To this day, the limited representation of women in mainstream media puts pressure on all women to conform to one standard of beauty regardless of their age, body type or skin colour. When inevitably the vast majority of us fall short, we feel inadequate, with potentially destructive consequences.

What happens when society's understanding and expectations of beauty – male and female – become impossible for all but the smallest proportion of us to achieve? The widespread loss of an individual's self-esteem.

High self-esteem allows us to value and accept ourselves warts and all, and it gives us strong coping skills when faced with life's challenges. Low self-esteem on the other hand leaves us vulnerable to the unrealistic societal expectations about beauty that we encounter everyday. Depression, eating disorders, cosmetic surgery and other interventions such as Botox are all products of low self-esteem.

Despite this bleak outlook and the sense that few corners of the world still exist where fashion and its media do not reach, there is a growing movement within the fashion industry to put greater emphasis on difference. All Walks Beyond the Catwalk is an organisation founded in London in May 2009 by top model Erin O'Connor, fashion broadcaster Caryn Franklin and fashion consultant Debra Bourne. Their goal was to kick-start an initiative dedicated to promoting diversity within the fashion industry. As a message from O'Connor and Franklin on the organization's website reads:

'WE LOVE FASHION IN ALL SHAPES AND SIZES. LIKE THE MULTITUDE OF SILHOUETTES AND GARMENTS OUR INDUSTRY BOTH PRODUCES AND PROMOTES, BEAUTY IS ALSO INDIVIDUAL. IT'S NOT RESTRICTED BY RACE, SHAPE, AGE OR SIZE.'

Most fashion insiders remain unwilling to take responsibility for the dangerous game being played with self-esteem, so it is encouraging that some advocates for change are speaking out from within the industry – it is these individuals who have the influence to make a real difference. Fashion itself gives us another means to fight back. We all know that finding the perfect outfit is a fast fix to increased self-confidence and can make us feel more attractive and secure in ourselves. The fashion industry should remember this: fashion has the power to make us feel *good* about ourselves. Imagine if the messages that greeted us every time we opened up a fashion magazine were diverse and overwhelmingly positive – how different would we feel?

# BIODEGRADABLE BIO-PLASTIC STILETTOS

## 70

In his 1933 publication *Footwear down the Ages*, Ernest Bordoli devoted a section to the 'achievement of the British boot manufacturing industry' during the First World War, which begins by asking, 'How many of my readers fully grasp what is meant by the making of 2,500,000 pairs of army boots?' It then proceeds to outline the staggering quantity of resources necessary for their manufacture: 'It requires 17 million square feet of leather equal to 400 acres; 4,000 tons of sole leather; 1,150 tons of metal for nailing the soles and heels, more than sufficient with which to build two fair-sized torpedo boat destroyers; 55 tons of thread and 78,000,000 eyelets. . . . To supply the order named above, 380,000 cattle had to be destroyed.'

Times have changed but the above facts offer a useful snapshot with which to ballpark the quantity of resources used to manufacture the millions of shoes and boots produced every day for luxury brands such as Prada and Jimmy Choo, fast-fashion retailers such as Aldo and Office, and sportswear brands such as Nike and Adidas. Synthetic imitation leather may now rival real leather as the basis for many of our shoes but we still use metal in the construction of stilettos, while studs, thread, laces and eyelets remain component parts.

OUT OF EVERYTHING WE WEAR, OUR SHOES ARE SUBJECT TO THE HARSHEST TREATMENT. WE WALK MILES IN THEM. THE LIFESPAN OF GOOD-QUALITY SHOES CAN BE EXTENDED WITH REGULAR VISITS TO THE COBBLER BUT EVEN SO HEELS WEAR DOWN, LEATHER LOOSENS AND STITCHING FRAYS.

For this reason, second-hand shoes are much less popular than second-hand clothes. Unfortunately, shoes are also more difficult to recycle because of the glues holding them together and their complex construction. Shoe manufacturers are trying to make a difference. Nike established their ReUSE A SHOE programme in 1990 and so far has recycled more than twenty-five million sports shoes into synthetic turf fields and sports surfaces. Converse joined this programme in 2011. Puma's Bring Me Back programme operates similarly and is officially Cradle to Cradle Certified. In 2012 Puma partnered up with Stella McCartney to launch a biodegradable range of shoes made of bio-plastics, which come from renewable raw materials.

# 71

# FACT:
# PRODUCTION
# STANDARDS

There are essentially three production standards in the fashion industry's supply chain. The first is the conventional system with all its accompanying issues with labour rights and exploitation. The second is ethical production where companies sign up and commit to set industry standards, such as the Ethical Trading Initiative, which aim to protect workers and improve factory conditions. Finally, there is Fair Trade, which guarantees that producers have received a living income from their work regardless of fluctuations in the market price. This means that individuals from poor and marginalized communities skilled in, for example, hand-weaving or embroidery have been paid thirty per cent more for their products than the market value. Profits are reinvested into community projects such as schools, water initiatives and micro-credit schemes.

# OUR FASHION FOOTPRINT

## 72

When considering our impact on the environment, the focus tends to be on our carbon footprint: our impact in terms of energy consumption. But what about our cultural footprint? Whether it is the books we read, the music we listen to, the films we watch or the clothes we wear, we are constantly developing our own social, cultural and political ideas and ideals. Your cultural footprint is the sum total of your cultural input and output. It expresses who you are in very real terms. Your cultural footprint is most easy to visualize in the context of the Internet. Online, our physical location and the geography that surrounds us become irrelevant to our daily social and cultural interactions, while our interests, values and cultural assumptions continue to occupy 'space' and exert influence.

The cultural footprint of the West is the biggest footprint of them all and in the world of fashion it is ever on the march. From Rio de Janeiro to New York, Paris to Beijing, Dubai to Melbourne, every fashion retailer and brand aspires to have a global presence. TopShop has opened in New York, Mulberry in China, Jaeger in Dubai – all three started in the United Kingdom. The ubiquity of designer brands and the fashion media that promote them seems to have no bounds; for example, there are twenty national editions of *Vogue* and twenty-eight of *Harper's Bazaar*, all supported by extensive websites. Location becomes irrelevant when individuals can network and share ideas through blogs, websites and interest groups.

The danger of bland homogeneity is increasing. Globally, we seem to have so much choice and yet we are in danger of losing our national and cultural identities as well as our own personal style and individuality. We are being encouraged to accept one culturally acceptable look. Will we forget that our cultural engagement with clothes is also part of who we are?

# HOW VERY BRITISH OF YOU

**73** Alexander McQueen was a master at drawing on his British heritage for inspiration. His ability to mix superb design and originality of thought with pattern-cutting and tailoring expertise gave an edginess to his fashion that was both original and distinctly British. He was at the forefront of a new conception of fashion and helped to put the United Kingdom on the international fashion circuit. McQueen's last, posthumous collection in Paris demonstrated how much of a loss his death was to fashion: the latest digital printing techniques re-imagining fourteenth-century religious iconography, the exquisite pattern cutting, the colours and fabrics, the silhouettes – all these touches made it so completely contemporary.

It was McQueen who described British fashion as being 'self-confident and fearless'. He said: 'It refuses to bow to commerce, thus generating a constant flow of new ideas while drawing on British heritage.' The British approach to fashion, creativity and new ideas is a mix of the entrepreneurial, the inventive and an at times idiosyncratic approach to the creation of new artefacts, products and works of art. These qualities generate new ideas in not only fashion but also all aspects of the creative and cultural industries. The British have an instinct for taking their physical heritage, as found in museums, architecture and the landscape, and combining it with the cultural developments of the present. The United Kingdom has never been a homogenous nation and continues to benefit from new immigrants, many of whom often become integral to the design, construction and making of British fashion.

# A CONVENIENT COINCIDENCE

**74** Fashion is full of contradictions. As individuals we try simultaneously both to stand out and blend in. We want to be ahead of the fashion curve yet not so far ahead that we look strange. Fashion-forward, not fashion victim, is the goal.

The industry's structure has its complications too. In theory every designer is pursuing his or her own vision when designing a collection and yet every season similar trends pop up on catwalks across the world. Is this synchronicity a case of the hive mentality in action? When designers dip into the collective cultural consciousness does it really whisper back to all of them, yes, florals and leather are where it is at this season? That is one possibility but, equally, narrowing and reducing what can be defined as fashionable ensures the industry's bottom line in a way that unlimited fashion trends do not. It's a convenient coincidence.

Technology and its creation of an ever-increasing number of fashion-savvy, international consumers have led to further contradictions. The Internet has made geography and the seasons irrelevant. Online, fashion is expected to evolve 24 hours a day, 365 days a year – and crucially it can. With capsule collections, collaborations between designers and retailers, pre-collections, resort collections, short runs and limited editions, the world of fashion is churning out new looks and styles at an unprecedented rate. Online shopping throws into relief the reality that every day it is summer and winter somewhere in the world. If you can buy any item of clothing at any time and have it delivered to any part of the world, how long can the seasonal model of the fashion industry endure? How can we be sure that what is in fashion now will still be in fashion tomorrow? And just what does being fashionable mean?

# FASHION EDUCATION TAKES FLIGHT

**75** Students arrive at the London College of Fashion enthusiastic, ambitious and hugely informed. In the past decade, the Internet has ushered in the democratization of fashion, opening up to the outside world any number of different channels to learn about, engage with and even shape the industry. The current generation of fashion students have grown up taking for granted instant access and insight into what was previously an aloof and restricted world glimpsed only in the pages of glossy magazines. Now the latest fashion shows are streamed live online, regular Tweets arrive on phones from industry insiders, and bloggers have as much influence as established critics. Anyone anywhere with an Internet connection has unprecedented access to the action. It's no wonder that many of my London College of Fashion students arrive experts, already actively involved in the creation as well as the consumption of fashion.

So why, when the online world offers so much, are these students still leaving their homes to study and train at an institution such as London College of Fashion? And in increasing numbers? As a fashion educator, I feel it is all about the need for context, community and concrete skills. Dedicated fashion degrees and diplomas, whether creative, practical, historical or business-focused, offer students something the Internet and media cannot: a critically engaged overview of the industry, technical skills of the highest standards, a learning environment of like-minded peers and staff, and opportunities to explore and discuss different regional, national and international perspectives, cultures and experiences.

Fashion educators are at the hard edge of understanding and making sense of the evolution of the fashion industry and how the latest global and technological changes will affect its future. In many ways, I sometimes feel we are building the plane while flying it.

# QUESTION: NEEDS VS. WANTS

How often do we convince ourselves that we *need* something when really we just *want* it and we want it only because it's currently fashionable?

# THE FASHION DESIGNER AS ARTIST

**77** Cultural critics often disagree on whether high fashion is an art or a craft. For me, it ultimately comes down to the motivations and conceptual thinking of the designer during the creative process, and while fashion can be art, more often than not it is a craft.

Yohji Yamamoto is one of the true designer–artists. He is frequently described as a designers' designer but for me that still underplays the significance of his work: Yamamoto is an artist who just happens to express himself through the medium of fashion. Like all great art, his garments bring together a number of unrelated concepts and then turn them on their head.

His approach to fashion has parallels with the thinking of artists working in other media. Zaha Hadid, for one, also works within the confines of an applied art. Yet architecture like fashion is full of artistic potential; it is all about volume, shape and engineering. Without these features neither buildings nor clothes could hang together or achieve aesthetic integrity. Think also of the artist Mark Rothko whose approach to blocked colour finds another articulation in Yamamoto's infinite shades of black, which the designer favours since black ensures no unintended meaning or emotions become associated with his clothes. Think of Samuel Beckett's minimalism and antipathy towards convention and then think of how Yamamoto has similarly challenged the established language of fashion, filtering out all unnecessary elements and embellishments so that we are forced to reconsider how and why clothes indicate aspects of our gender, body shape or personality.

Yamamoto's designs have a function beyond fashion and always push our ideas about what clothes can be to the edge. They have a timelessness that makes them anomalous in an industry that insists on a constant turnover of trends. Never divorced entirely from past or present understandings of fashion – whether Western or Japanese – they nevertheless point unequivocally to the future and to new ways of understanding clothing. Wim Wenders, the German director behind the 1989 documentary devoted to Yamamoto, *Notebook on Cities and Clothes*, has said of the designs: 'The clothes are new, but when you put them on you feel as though you have been wearing them for years; they are like a second skin.' A Yamamoto garment will still look current some five or ten years after it first appeared on the catwalk.

Yamamoto has described his clothes as being without nationality but there can be little doubt that his Japanese heritage contributes to his visionary deconstruction of Western dress conventions and his re-imagining of masculine tailoring for the female form. Fabric has been central to his work from the outset and he works closely with small-scale producers of craft textiles in Japan. Every collection bears evidence of his intuitive understanding of a textile's ability to embody a garment, give strength to a fragile frame or shape a wearer. As Yamamoto himself has said, technique comes second. First, he must be struck by something beautiful, then an appreciation of shape or volume will follow and ultimately that will determine how he arranges the fabric and whether he uses darts or hems.

Yamamoto believes that perfection is ugly; that it is scars, failures and disorder that advance creativity and originality, rather like how grit in an oyster ends up a pearl. Yamamoto sums up his creative motivations best:

'What I have longed to create, what I have believed in, what I have dedicated my life to is that formless something floating in the mist. That mysterious something can be intuited only through the miraculous sensibilities with which humans have been endowed. It is pre-lingual, it can only be labelled an intangible asset.'

# WHEREBY FASHION AND DEATH HAVE A FRIENDLY CHAT

**78** In his essay 'A Dialogue between Fashion and Death', the poet and philosopher Giacomo Leopardi imagines a discussion in which Fashion attempts to convince Death that they are so similar they might as well be sisters. Fashion points out 'that it is our nature and our custom to keep renovating the world', continuing, 'I persuade and force all genteel men to endure daily a thousand hardships and a thousand discomforts and often pain and torment and I even get some of them to die gloriously for love of me.'

Leopardi died in 1837 and the fashionable torments and discomforts endured by the style-conscious individuals of his day are a long cry from those around now. Still, I feel an affinity with Leopardi. I too sometimes cast my arms up in the air at the utter impracticality of the clothes and shoes that come down the runway some seasons. And yet I love fashion too. At least we can take comfort in the fact that even some one hundred and fifty years ago fashionistas had more style than sense.

# NOT ANY OLD FISH IN THE SEA

**79** Diana Vreeland, Coco Chanel, the Duchess of Windsor, Cate Blanchett, Charlotte Rampling, Tilda Swinton – these are women who all possess or possessed a strong personal style that set them apart from the merely fashionable.

Style is about personality. It is about striking a pose that says something about you and not about the clothes. It is about daring to mix periods, labels and designers when putting together the perfect statement outfit. It is not about buying a complete outfit that someone else chose for you.

To develop your own personal style you will need to start by making your own decisions and thinking carefully about your purchases. You can still be inspired by the latest designer collection but that doesn't mean you have to buy it hook, line and sinker.

# RETAIL RETROFIT

**80** In his 1883 novel *The Ladies' Paradise*, French author Émile Zola wrote of the rise of a *grand magasin*, or department store, in Paris and the disastrous repercussions its success had on the small drapers and haberdashers nearby. Zola's self-professed goal was to 'write the poem of modern life' and dense descriptions of the store and its strategies of seduction – advertising, scents and experiences – recur throughout.

The arrival of the *grand magasin* in the nineteenth century inaugurated the dawn of modern retail. Whether browsing or buying, the experience of visiting a department store fulfilled a very human desire to explore and try something new. Over a century later, the important role that such stores play in our lives has diminished (though John Lewis and Nordstrom still remain beloved thanks in no small part to their hugely well-informed floor staff). Today it is the flagship store taking retail to the next level. Louis Vuitton on London's Bond Street, the Prada flagship in Tokyo, a Comme des Garçons concept store in Beijing – these are the twenty-first century's answer to Zola's temples of consumption.

International luxury powerhouses are at the forefront of pioneering new, innovative retail experiences. In multi-storey, architecturally designed interiors, art installation, live performance, video and in-house ateliers now sit alongside clothes, perfumes, beauty products, jewelry, bags and other accessories. Take Burberry's flagship store on London's Regent Street as an example. It features interactive mirrors that, unprompted, transform into video screens showing footage of the garment that you've just tried on as it appeared on the catwalk (radio chips attached to the garment cue this magic). 'Choreographed audio-visual takeovers' occur throughout the day, during which lights darken and screens light up with fashion films, 'seamlessly blurring physical and digital worlds'. Tills are nowhere to be found since, as in Apple stores, payment comes to you in the form of a gracious salesperson and a portable swipe machine. Is this the future of retail?

The shop is evolving yet again. Who can predict what form our 'poem of modern life' will take in ten years time?

# THE LANGUAGE OF OUR CLOTHES

**81** Just as it takes time to develop a complete vocabulary and total command of grammar and syntax, so too it takes time to master the language of clothes. Remember those early attempts to dress yourself free from a parent's watchful eye? Or all those fashion mishaps of your teen years? They were part of the learning curve through which you came to know instinctively that certain garments are to be worn at certain times, in a certain order and in a certain configuration.

WE EVOLVE A LANGUAGE OF CLOTHES JUST AS WE EVOLVE SPEECH PATTERNS, TRYING OUT NEW CLOTHES THE SAME AS WE TRY OUT NEW WORDS.

But how articulate do we ever become? I wonder if the psychotherapist Adam Phillips got it right when he speculated, 'The words we can never use might be like the clothes we can never wear.'

# CHOICE, GLORIOUS CHOICE

**82** With too much choice, all choices become equal. As the philosopher Albert Camus asked: 'Should I kill myself or have a cup of coffee?' This quote is one of my favourites because it says everything about how inured we have become to choice. Choice has pervaded our lives to such an extent that simply buying a pair of jeans, a T-shirt or even a pair of socks can become overwhelming. Is too much choice the reason why some of us dress so badly? It seems as if our ability to be expressive with our clothes diminishes, as our options increase. Perhaps choice is inflicting a slow sartorial death upon us all.

'Choice', as the American psychologist Barry Schwartz describes it, 'has a clear and powerful instrumental value; it enables people to get what they need and want in life. . . . Choice is what enables each person to pursue precisely those objects that best satisfy his or her own preference within the limits of his or her financial resources.' Capitalism has delivered choice with an ever-increasing range of goods and services. Our predilection for choosing has driven and is driving the development of economies around the world.

> BUYING FASHIONABLE GOODS IS AT ITS CORE AN EXERCISE IN DISCERNMENT AND CHOICE.

Around the world, we humans have been hugely creative in satisfying our addiction to choice. Can we now be equally creative in finding solutions to the consequences?

# LEATHER HIDES

**83** Wearing animal skins is no longer necessary in the twenty-first century. Contemporary fibres are just as effective at keeping our bodies warm, and a range of new materials can protect our feet equally well. Yet we immediately respond to leather in terms of its quality, tactility and flexibility. Most of us have a key leather item in our wardrobes, whether a dress, skirt or the ubiquitous biker jacket.

Humans have converted animal skins and hides into leather for millennia, and today leather remains worn by the vast majority of people, who consider it more ethically acceptable than fur. As with most ethical questions, however, answers are never straightforward. The leather-processing industry promotes leather as an environmentally friendly by-product of the meat industry. The skins of cattle, sheep and goats reared for their meat, milk or wool would be treated as a waste product were it not for the leather industry. Yet, in reality only twenty to thirty per cent of an animal hide is converted into leather, with the remainder generally thrown away. During the complex, multi-stage manufacturing process, the skins also undergo severe biological, chemical and mechanical treatments – for example, salt and sulphide treatments – mostly in huge vats of water that leave behind contaminated wastewaters and effluents containing high levels of harmful pollutants, including unusable hide, flesh and other solid waste, which must be collected and discarded.

More stringent regulation is putting pressure on the leather-processing industry to reduce its impact on the environment. New processes and technologies aim to reduce the levels of harmful pollutants within wastewater and to improve treatment technologies and water disposal methods, but these are still in early stages. As consumers of leather, we too need to do our part by asking fashion houses and retailers what they are doing to improve the manufacturing processes. Their waste is our waste.

# A SENSE OF
# BELONGING(S)

**84** Since 2005, the Chinese photographers Huang Quingjun and Ma Hongjie have been collaborating on *Family Stuff*, a photographic series that documents the possessions of people across China. Huang and Ma work independently – covering the north and south of China respectively – but their photographs always feature similar tableaux: individuals or families standing outside where they live with all their belongings arranged around them. Each photograph poignantly captures, regardless of what is on display, our very human attachment to our possessions. Whether featuring a nomadic family with a satellite TV or a single man with every available gadget, the photographs reveal what is important to these individuals and how they choose to spend their income. Clothes are among the possessions documented in this project but they are rarely centre stage.

If you were to pull out from your wardrobe all your clothing and accessories and arrange them around you, what do you think that image might reveal? What if you had to divide your clothes into two piles: those articles you wear regularly and those you wear only rarely? Which pile would be bigger? If the latter, would you feel uncomfortable faced with all these unwanted, unneeded clothes? Or would you regard them as a badge of honour – a totem to the level of your disposable income? What if you were asked to pile up only those garments that you love – the ones you've saved for their memories even though they no longer fit or have begun to fall apart?

Now imagine how the world would read this portrait of you. What conclusions would be drawn upon seeing you there, standing alone among all your clothes? What predilections for colour or black or stripes might come to the fore? What obsessions might be revealed? What interests or hobbies?

Now imagine how *you* would respond to this self-portrait. What sartorial mistakes would you shake your head at? Would you determine to donate all those unworn clothes to charity shops, friends or family? Would you resolve to think more carefully about what you buy? To put greater care and attention into your purchases?

# INDUSTRIAL EVOLUTION

## 85

Over the centuries, the latest technologies, media developments and labour movements have contributed to the transformation of the fashion industry. Examples include sewing machines, immigrant tailors, the department store, ready-to-wear collections, the printing of fashion images and the fashion magazine.

Fashion has moved from handmade craftsmanship designed and constructed for society's elite to a global industry based on mass production and dominated by the power of the consumer and the latest technologies.

# THE EMPORIUM STRIKES BACK

**86** Who will be the last one standing? Net-A-Porter.com or Saks Fifth Avenue? Asos.com or TopShop? Digital evangelists would have us believe that it has got to be one or the other, and in their minds digital is the inevitable victor, but the reality is it's not a zero-sum game. Online retailers are interested in expanding into bricks-and-mortar shops while bricks-and-mortar shops are developing online retail sites. It's not 'either/or' but yes to both channels.

Importantly, the physical shop remains more profitable than online retail, a point that *The Economist* stressed in a July 2013 article (from which I borrowed the clever title for this entry). For this reason, both retailers with growing online sales and online retailers remain interested in the physical shop.

The shop as showroom is one future being bandied about. The shop as glorified change room is another: order clothes online to try on in store and if they don't fit, return them there and then. Those retail innovations that I discussed earlier (see pp.108–9) are also bound to roll out in more and more shops. The shop re-imagined as an immersive experience or adventure may keep it relevant more than anything else.

# 87

## FACT: CLOTHING VALUES

The clothes of an average British household have produced carbon emissions equivalent to driving the average modern car some six thousand miles and have consumed enough water to fill a thousand bathtubs to capacity. Yet thirty per cent of these clothes are rarely, if ever, worn. A survey of fifteen thousand people in fifteen countries in both the northern and southern hemispheres found water scarcity and water pollution as their top two environmental concerns. We need to start making the connection between what we value and what we wear sooner rather than later.

# THE
# CAPPUCCINO
# EFFECT

**88** When talking about the significance of good design, a colleague of mine often refers to 'the cappuccino effect'. Why are people prepared to pay double, triple, even quadruple for a cappuccino instead of opting for a cheap instant coffee served in a plastic cup with powdered milk? My colleague explains that it all comes down to design-thinking, or 'the cappuccino effect'. We are willing to spend far more for a cappuccino because of all that accompanies it: the origin and quality of the beans; the sophisticated espresso machine; the stylish cup and saucer; perhaps even the fact that you get a small biscotti as a bonus. Design-thinking can be intangible too. The perceived talent of the barista or the attentiveness of a waiter could also be contributing factors to the decision to skip the instant option.

How and in what form a product arrives with us is often just as important in our decision to purchase it as the product itself. Apple's attention to detail in its packaging and product design makes the iPhone a must-have gadget. Design-thinking gives a product its edge. It is what makes certain brands, shops and garments fashionable, and is the difference between the everyday and the extraordinary. It explains why a basic T-shirt can be transformed into one that commands a designer price tag. It lies behind the decision to select one fabric over another and update a shirt with an unusual collar shape or sleeve length.

Many countries are keen to kick-start and sustain economic growth through design-thinking. Founding and supporting national art and design institutions and curricula is a good place to start. Harnessing design-thinking can transform a country from a manufacturing hub into a design *and* manufacturing hub, which crucially will export its goods around the world.

# AFRICAN STYLE

**89** Africa has a diverse variety of national and tribal dress, some of which combine traditional patterns, colours and textiles with European garments introduced during the colonization of the continent. The integration of these very different aesthetics and cultural approaches to dress has resulted in utterly unique styles. Members of the Herero tribe of Namibia, for example, wear beautifully cut and tailored dresses, trousers and shirts that resemble those late Victorian styles worn by European missionaries and by later settlers during the German colonial rule of the country. These classic cuts are worn by the Herero tribe in exuberant, colourful fabrics, making for a surprising combination of two almost contradictory aesthetic forces.

North of Namibia, in the Bakongo district of Brazzaville, Republic of Congo, Western dress has been similarly re-imagined by the Sapeurs, men who belong to the Society for the Advancement of People of Elegance, which is dedicated to all matters sartorial. The Sapeurs are all stunningly well dressed in three-piece suits and carefully selected ties and fedoras. Their dandyish attire began as a passive form of resistance against President Mobutu Sese Seko's attempts to rid the country of all Western cultural influences in the 1960s and 1970s. Two examples from a continent as diverse as Africa can never approximate the whole story but what I find particularly interesting is how these two communities have combined a range of references to construct their own empowering approaches to dress.

THIS IS HOW EVERYONE – ACROSS THE GLOBE – SHOULD BE APPROACHING FASHION: AS AN OPPORTUNITY FOR DISPLAY, CREATIVITY AND INDIVIDUALITY.

# FASHION AS SCULPTURE

**90** Today the sculptural potential of fashion is often overlooked in favour of figure-hugging designs that curve around the human form. But despite the triumph of form-fitting fashions, there remains a number of highly influential designers whose designs make the sculptural and architectural qualities of fashion clear. Rei Kawakubo of Comme des Garçons, Yohji Yamamoto, Alexander McQueen, Hussein Chalayan, Boudicca – these designers all give real expression to the structural nature of fashion with designs that embrace fresh new angles, shapes and planes that are entirely foreign but still complementary to the human body.

# HOW MUCH
# IS TOO MUCH?

**91** A Bugatti Veyron sports car costs $2.6 million; a Louis Moinet Meteoris watch costs $4.6 million; a penthouse flat in Monaco reaches $280 million; and a parking place in central London fetches $480,000. With these prices in the back of your mind, you can begin to understand how, for the world's wealthiest, a designer handbag costing $36,000 or a couture dress at $50,000 might look like reasonable purchases.

Some of these exorbitant prices do have justification in reality. It takes Hermès five to seven years to train the craftspeople making their leather handbags and the prices reflect that investment. Just as the technology in the latest $1.38 million Maybach Landaulet works it way through the car industry to the lower priced Nissan Micra or Ford Focus, so too the skills and crafts pioneered by luxury brands ultimately find their way into the fashion food chain. When costing luxury goods, a portion of the price is set aside to invest in such skills development and research. It is still true that most of the mark-up on these luxury goods goes to pure, over-the-top profits, but on a percentage basis, profits in fashion are usually equal to those generated by any other product or gadget.

Prices are increasing, however, and more and more I do wonder how much is too much? Is there a ceiling on how high prices can go? Since luxury goods now seem predominantly to be identified by their price tags – the higher the price, the more exclusive the product – I suspect not.

# 92

# RUBBISH
# QUESTIONS

Is the amount of rubbish we generate a fair indication of how much we consume?

Is the amount of rubbish in our wardrobes an indication of our indecisiveness?

Or do we make bad choices because we are rubbish at shopping?

# THE TALENT
# INCUBATOR

**93** London is often cited as the city that most effectively supports and generates new fashion talent. Why is this? Its fashion ecosystem is certainly unique and thriving but the ecosystems of Paris, New York, Hong Kong and Tokyo are too, in their own way. London is a creative hub, yes, with an established and respected network of art schools that train and develop talent for the creative and cultural industries. The city also benefits from a cultural rebelliousness that leads young talent to resist the status quo and take risks, to speculate and ask 'What if?'

All of the above is true. What I have learned though is that all of this creativity and entrepreneurialism needs an infrastructure to support it. Leaving young fashion businesses to battle it out in a game of survival of the fittest is not the answer. Instead, careful and considered incubation at every stage will see these businesses grow and flourish. This is what has made the difference in London.

As London-based fashion graduates embark on their careers, they can take advantage of any number of initiatives. The Centre for Fashion Enterprise offers young designers affordable studio spaces, advice on business, production and manufacturing, and help in showcasing their collections at London Fashion Week. Since 1993 the British Fashion Council's NEWGEN scheme has awarded young designers sizeable prize monies to help them develop collections, and slots on the London Fashion Week schedule. A list of past NEWGEN recipients reads like a roll call for the best of British fashion and includes

Alexander McQueen, Boudicca, Matthew Williamson, Christopher Kane, Erdem and Mary Katrantzou. The annual Fashion Fringe award, founded by Colin McDowell and IMG in 2003, aims to foster originality and innovation in fashion by providing a cutting-edge designer with financial support, mentoring and a showcase at London Fashion Week. Other events tied to the promotion of emerging talent in London include Fashion East and Vauxhall Fashion Scout.

All of these structures have worked together to make London a hotbed for creative talent. Cities around the world take note.

# GLOVES

## 94

Thinking about some of the historical protocols related to clothes, it is remarkable how far we have come in relaxing certain social norms. Take gloves. From the outset, gloves were more than a protective necessity. For the upper classes, they were a badge of distinction, more meaningful than any old fashion statement. Gloves played a key role in settling a contract or in provoking an altercation. For almost eight hundred years, English law enshrined the act of throwing one's glove to the ground as the accepted incitement to a duel. Liturgical gloves were symbols of rank within the Church and worn only by bishops, cardinals and the pope.

Gloves made for a highly prized, costly gift, especially those that were heavily jewelled and embroidered. Queen Elizabeth I had two thousand pairs of gloves and a dedicated wardrobe mistress to look after them. Until the nineteenth century, upper-class Europeans wore gloves at all times. It was considered improper for a woman even to partly remove her gloves in public. Into the 1950s, well-to-do women were still expected to wear gloves whenever they left the home.

> For centuries, gloves were an indispensable accessory. Now, we only wear them in cold weather or for other practical reasons. What happened? It is fair to say that central heating, cars and other innovations played their part but still for something that was so integral to our formal way of life to have so fully fallen out of fashion is thought provoking.

It is only in language that we still find relics of the profound role that gloves played in the past: throw down the gauntlet; iron fist in a velvet glove; hand in glove; fits like a glove.

# FRIDA KAHLO: STYLE ICON

## 95

When someone asks me who my favourite style icon is, I always initially think of fashion legends such as Diana Vreeland and Coco Chanel or a more contemporary woman, perhaps, such as the actresses Tilda Swinton or Chloë Sevigny. Then the Mexican artist Frida Khalo springs to mind and sticks. She is my style icon.

Why, you ask? In part, because of her vibrant uncompromising imagery, political commitment and strong sense of self, which have made her a constant source of inspiration for me and encouraged my lifelong commitment to feminism. The physical trauma that Kahlo endured so early on in her life shaped her. She did not consider becoming an artist until a near-fatal bus accident; thereafter she found in art a conduit through which to channel her pain and physical restrictions.

There is an intense and searing perception to a Frida Kahlo painting that I feel other artists fail to achieve. And, to me, Kahlo's unique sense of style has always been extraordinary and appealing. She used clothes, jewelry and the rituals of dress as an integral part of her imagery – in paintings and in life. How she chose to dress reflects how fashion and clothing connect us not only to our inner selves but also to the world around us. Her decision to style her hair in traditional plaits, her sartorial references to historical Mexican dress and her use of corsets to help manage her physical pain all became symbols of her determination and inner strength. Through her personal style, Frida Kahlo extended her artistic influence beyond art and into the theatre of life.

# IN PURSUIT OF FASHION IMMORTALITY

## 96

'The museum not only controls fashion immortality, it has become the launching pad for new styles inspired by the past,' wrote Joan Kron in her 1976 review of Diana Vreeland's 'American Women of Style' exhibition at the Metropolitan Museum's Costume Institute in New York. Vreeland, the hugely influential fashion editor, first at *Harper's Bazaar* and then *Vogue*, had become consultant curator to the Costume Institute in 1971. There she instigated what would become a global phenomenon – the museum fashion exhibition. Indeed, it could well be the greatest legacy of her long and varied career, for Vreeland understood that fashion was about so much more than just the clothes. Her exhibitions featured a range of artefacts and cultural objects that positioned the garments as physical manifestations of complex ideas and motivations either developed by a designer or part of a wider cultural movement.

AS THE SIGNIFICANCE OF FASHION AS AN INDUSTRY AND LIFESTYLE HAS GROWN, SO HAS THE POPULARITY OF THE FASHION EXHIBITION.

The 'blockbuster exhibition' is drawing in visitors to museums in record numbers and it seems every cultural institution is keen to add one to its annual programming. Exhibitions tend to focus either on an individual designer or fashion house, such as Andrew Bolton's hugely successful 'Savage Beauty' exhibition on Alexander McQueen at the Metropolitan Museum of Art, on a historical movement, such as Claire Wilcox's 'The Golden Age of Couture' at the Victoria and Albert Museum, or on the theory and conceptual underpinnings of fashion, as did Judith Clark's 'Dictionary of Dress' at London's Blythe House. These curators strove to capture the beauty and power of the clothes as well as the ideas and rationale behind them.

The fashion exhibition is not without controversy. Some intellectuals consider fashion too lightweight for the hallowed halls of the museum, while others frown on the involvement of fashion houses still in business, which sometimes seek to influence the curator's interpretation of its history and often donate large sums towards the exhibition's costs. These brands inevitably benefit commercially from the extensive press and marketing campaigns that accompany the shows. Vreeland herself was criticized for the design of an Yves Saint Laurent exhibition that too closely resembled the fashion house's in-store displays.

To me, such criticism misses the point. Fashion is a business, and selling and inspiring people to wear their clothes is the motivation of all designers. That holds true even when fashion is being displayed in a museum. The clothes may arguably be art, some may never have been worn, but they are still the output of a global industry.

# KARL LAGERFELD AND HIGH-TECH FUR

## 97

Why are fur sales rising?

In the 1980s, the case against fur was made so strongly that many in the fashion industry thought it could never make a comeback, not least because technology had developed that meant good-quality faux fur was more often than not being mistaken for real animal fur. As Karl Lagerfeld said in an interview with *Harper's Bazaar*: 'The material is beautiful, and new in a way, because it was not that perfect before. . . . Now the technology has advanced so much that you can hardly tell fake fur from the real thing.' Though editor Anna Wintour famously refused to give in to pressure to ban furs from the pages of *Vogue* (earning herself the reputation as

PETA's public enemy number one), a groundswell of anti-fur sentiment made it seem like long-lasting change was at hand.

> Fast-forward to 2009 and Naomi Campbell, icon of a 1990s anti-fur campaign – she famously appeared naked along with four other supermodels above the tagline 'We'd rather go naked than wear fur' – was modelling fur for luxury brand Dennis Basso and fur on the catwalks was raising far less ire than some ten years earlier. How did this happen?

Ironically, in the long run, the popularity of faux fur has made real fur more acceptable and more desirable. Designers' experimentation with both materials blurred the boundaries of what was and was not real. Dyed or styled animal furs might appear faux even as faux fur approximated the real thing. The vintage revival further complicated the debate as many consumers deemed the wearing of a vintage fur coat more acceptable than buying a new coat, whatever its material. You can understand their rationale: the animal was killed long ago and surely it is better to reuse a historical garment than to throw it away.

> Campaigns funded by fur producers have also had an effect. With worldwide sales of fur totalling $13 billion in 2008, the industry has taken pains to show how production methods have improved and to make an environmental case for fur. Factor in the expanding fashion markets in China and Russia, where wearing fur is more culturally acceptable, and in their climates more practical, and it is little wonder that demand for fur is on the rise.

In Scandinavia, Greenland, Russia and Iceland, where fur has always been a practical and essential item of clothing, furriers have worked to improve the living conditions of the animals and their means of death. They assure consumers that of all the animals killed for human use these have the best conditions, and argue that the animals that end up as leather bags or shoes, or even as meat cuts, have had worse living and end-of-life conditions than the ones reared only for clothing. Additionally, the farmers and workers involved with the skinning and treating of the pelts have better wages and living conditions than many of those individuals manufacturing other fashion products.

Animal husbandry is only one factor in the fur debate. Environmentally motivated accusations about energy use are also frequent – from both sides. While the American Fur Commission says it takes one gallon of oil to make just three fake-fur jackets, another study by the University of Michigan concluded that the energy necessary to produce a coat of ranch-raised animal furs is twenty times that required for a fake product. Furriers rebuff such conclusions by pointing out that, unlike fake fur, animal fur is biodegradable and these garments are looked after, cherished and handed down between family members, giving real fur strong environmental credentials. Animal activists in turn claim that chemicals applied during the treatment of pelts to stop rot render them no longer biodegradable. And so, the debate continues.

FOR ME, FUR GOES TO THE HEART OF THE PERSONAL AND ETHICAL DEBATE THAT EACH INDIVIDUAL NEEDS TO HAVE ABOUT HIS OR HER CLOTHES.

While it certainly provokes raw emotions, fur is not a black and white issue, nor is it an isolated one. If we are to question seriously the morals of the fur industry, we need to be consistent and question the means of production behind *every* garment we buy. Focusing on fur in isolation neglects the bigger picture. Whether it is water consumption, labour conditions, pollutants or the treatment of animals, it is up to us to put pressure on the fashion industry to take responsibility for how products are sourced and manufactured.

# AUTHENTICITY

**98** Flicking through a magazine, fashion can seem ephemeral, light-weight, even shallow, the antithesis of authentic. However, when you get beyond the glitz and celebrity coverage to meet the many people who create and work in this dynamic, creative industry, it soon becomes apparent that to have an impact authenticity is essential. Being passionate yet totally professional with a genuine desire to develop a unique vision and work hard is the only way to succeed.

# PUT YOURSELF
# IN THEIR SHOES

**99** From early childhood, our parents tell us, 'Put yourself in their shoes,' whenever we come down unfairly on our siblings, friends or classmates. Similarly, we are often told that someone has left very big shoes to fill as a means to illustrate the significance of their con-tribution. Shoes seem to have infiltrated our language more so than clothing, perhaps because it is our shoes that take such a pounding day in, day out.

These days, shoes allow us to move across any terrain and any eventuality can be catered for, whether it is a trip under the sea, to the moon or simply for a run. Shoes have been designed for every job and activity – lumberjacks, coal miners, sheep-shearers – and even for wearing in the fields to chop rice stubble. Thanks to the range of available footwear, we can work and move with freedom and safety.

# MANUFACTURING OPPORTUNITY

**00** For years, cheap labour and oil prices combined to make Asia the manufacturing hub of the world. That may begin to change over the next ten years. As the wages of skilled workers increase and oil prices continue to rise, the financial advantages of manufacturing overseas will begin to diminish for European and American retailers. Shifting the manufacturing of fashion back to domestic factories will offer each nation its own challenges and rewards. It will certainly make possible a much swifter turnaround between design and sales, a business model already proven by companies such as Zara and H&M, which, because they switch over their stock every six weeks, manufacture their garments as close to market as possible.

If basic economics brings manufacturing closer to home, governments will need to gain a better understanding of its country's design and production needs. The closer integration of design education, manufacturing skills and technological investment would be a good place to start.

# AN
# AFTERTHOUGHT

## 101

When it comes to our clothes, let's take inspiration from William Morris, the great nineteenth-century British designer and socialist, who got it exactly right when he wrote:

'HAVE NOTHING IN YOUR HOUSE THAT YOU DO NOT KNOW TO BE USEFUL, OR BELIEVE TO BE BEAUTIFUL.'

# ACKNOWLEDGMENTS

I would like to thank Jamie Camplin for seeing the potential in my thinking around the issues surrounding fashion and for commissioning this book.

I would also like to thank Laura Potter, who introduced me to the key, and at times mysterious, role of the editor.

I would particularly like to thank Rebecca Doolan, who undertook crucial research and initial proofing for me; Georgina Rusling for ensuring I had the time necessary to write; and Scarlett McGuire, who taught me so much about how to approach writing.

I would like to thank Laura Santamaria for inviting me to write for *Sublime Magazine* and for allowing me to rework and use some of my original columns here.

Thank you to Hannah Wood, Angela Lambert at Yohji Yamamoto, Nicola Bion and Lois McNay for all things fashion, friendship and feminist.

Above all, I would like to thank T.C. and Jacob for their constant patience, tolerance, humour and encouragement.

# FURTHER READING AND SELECTED SOURCES

Barnard, Malcolm, *Fashion as Communication*, London, 2002

Barthes, Roland, *The Fashion System*, tr. Matthew Ward and Richard Howard, Berkeley, [1968] 1983

——. *The Language of Fashion*, Andy Stafford (tr.) and Michael Carter, eds., Oxford and New York, 2006

Bartlett, Djurdja, *FashionEast: The Spectre that Haunted Socialism*, Cambridge, Mass., 2010

Black, Sandy, *The Sustainable Fashion Handbook*, London and New York, 2012

Brand, Jan, and José Teunissen, eds., *Global Fashion, Local Tradition: On the Globalisation of Fashion*, London, 2005

British Fashion Council, *Value of the UK Fashion Industry Report*, London, 2010

Buckley, Cheryl, and Hilary Fawcett, *Fashioning the Feminine: Representation and Women's Fashion from the Fin de Siècle to the Present*, London, 2001

Byrne Paquet, Laura, *The Urge to Splurge: A Social History of Shopping*, Toronto, 2003

Church Gibson, Pamela, *Fashion and Celebrity Culture*, Oxford and New York, 2011

Clark, Judith, and Adam Phillips, *The Concise Dictionary of Dress*, London, 2010

Clarke, Louise, ed., *The Measure*, London, 2008

Damhorst, Mary Lynn, and Susan B. Kaiser, eds., *Critical Linkages in Textiles and Clothing Subject Matter*, Knoxville, 1991

Davis, Fred, *Fashion, Culture and Identity*, Chicago, 1994

Department for Environment, Food & Rural Affairs, *Sustainable Clothing Action Plan*, London, 2011

Entwistle, Joanne, *The Fashioned Body: Fashion, Dress and Modern Social Theory*, London, 2000

Fletcher, Kate, and Lynda Grose, *Fashion & Sustainability: Design for Change*, London, 2012

Geczy, Adam, and Vicki Karaminas, *Fashion and Art*, Oxford, 2012

Grant, Linda, *The Thoughtful Dresser*, London, 2009

Institute for Manufacturing, University of Cambridge, *Well Dressed? The Present and Future Sustainability of Clothing and Textiles in the United Kingdom*, Cambridge, 2006

Kawamura, Yuniya, *Fashion-ology*, Oxford and New York, 2005

Laver, James, *Costume and Fashion: A Concise History*, 5th edition, London, 2002

McDowell, Colin, *Literary Companion to Fashion*, London, 1995

Morganroth Gullette, Margaret, *Aged by Culture*, Chicago, 2004

Pickett, Kate, and Richard Wilkinson, *The Spirit Level: Why Greater Equality Makes Societies Stronger*, London, 2009

Schor, Juliet, *The Overspent American: Upscaling, Downshifting and the New Consumer*, New York and London, 1999

Schwartz, Barry, *The Paradox of Choice: Why More is Less*, New York and London, 2004

Walter, Natasha, *Living Dolls: The Return of Sexism*, London, 2010

World Wildlife Fund, *Deeper Luxury Report*, London, 2007

——. *Living Planet Report*, London 2012

# RELEVANT WEBSITES

www.britishfashioncouncil.co.uk

www.businessoffashion.com

www.dazeddigital.com

www.drapersonline.com

www.ecofashionworld.com

www.ecotextile.com

# INDEX

**FRANCES CORNER** is Head of London College of Fashion, a role she has held since 2005. She sits on the British Fashion Council's Advisory Board and the Executive Committee of the International Foundation of Fashion Technology Institutes. She holds a DPhil from Oxford University, writes widely on art and design education, and regularly advises stakeholders on the fashion industry.

First published in the United Kingdom in 2014 by Thames & Hudson Ltd, 181A High Holborn, London WC1V 7QX

*Why Fashion Matters* © 2014 Frances Corner

Designed by Material Organisation
Photo: Hill & Aubrey

British Library Cataloguing-in-Publication Data
A catalogue record for this book is available from the British Library

ISBN 978-0-500-51737-6

Printed and bound in China by C&C Offset Printing Co Ltd

To find out about all our publications, please visit **www.thamesandhudson.com**. There you can subscribe to our e-newsletter, browse or download our current catalogue, and buy any titles that are in print.